C Struik (Pty) Limited 56 Wale Street Cape Town
First edition 1976
Copyright © 1976 Gerald Cubitt and Johann Richter

ISBN 0 86977 075 6

Art direction and design by Willem Jordaan Cape Town
Lithographic reproduction by Unifoto (Pty) Limited Cape Town
Photoset by McManus Bros (Pty) Limited Cape Town
Printed and bound by Printpak (Cape) Limited Cape Town

List of sources
All photographs which appear in this book were taken
by Gerald Cubitt with the exception of the following:
Anthony Bannister 1 34 35 50 100 101 105 123 125 126 142 185 205
Cosint Costruzioni Internazionali SPA 93 95
Gordon Douglas 49 222
Peter Johnson 24 25 103 138 144 177 178 179 180 183 184 188 219 230
Harald Pager 128

Gerald Cubitt Johann Richter

SouthWest

There is a vast land sprawled along southern Africa's Atlantic seaboard astride the Tropic of Capricorn. In the east it is bounded by desert wasteland; in the west by the shifting Namib sands; and in the south by scrubland and rocky plains. Only in the north has Nature been less severe. Here the serene Okavango flows through wooded savannah, eventually to seep away beneath the Kalahari. In this mystic land man and beast, flora and fauna, have somehow managed to survive and multiply in precarious interdependence. To me this has always been an enchanted place, a place to capture the spirit, and I have returned there again and again. Now more than ever before it is also a land of contrasts, where jack-hammers shatter the desert silence and primitive rhythms mingle with the whine of jet engines. The cosmopolitan crowds of Windhoek's Kaiserstrasse are aeons removed from the ghosts that walk the lonely Skeleton Coast. It has been given many names: The land God made in anger; The ageless land. Today it is known only by its geographic location: South West Africa.   Johann Richter Cape Town April 1976

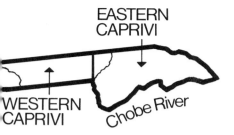

EASTERN CAPRIVI

WESTERN CAPRIVI

Chobe River

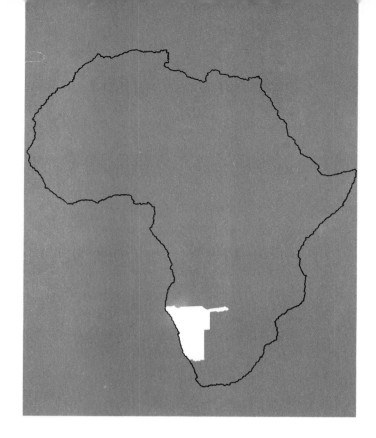

South West Africa

Exploration of the African coast in the 15th century was originally inspired by Christianity and the desire for trade. In medieval times merchandise from the East had been brought by dangerous overland routes through Asia Minor to the Mediterranean trading centres, but the conflict between Christianity and Islam stimulated a search for alternative routes. The direction these took was based on the grand medieval misconception that the African coast flattened out south of the then known Ivory Coast. Navigators believed that by sailing along this coast they would find the legendary Christian kingdom of Ethiopia: and they were convinced that by sailing still further east, India and its fabulous riches would be reached.

The Portuguese, a small but industrious nation, were among the leading traders on the Continent and first to explore beyond the known horizons. Imbued with a burning zeal to spread Christianity, the pious Infante Dom Henrique, 'Henry the Navigator', planned expeditionary fleets to win the support of Prester John,

Emperor of Ethiopia, in the struggle against the Turkish menace. In the process he also hoped to secure the riches of the Orient. By the time of his death his fleets had travelled down the west coast of Africa and reached the present-day Gulf of Guinea. There the lucrative trade in tropical goods and slaves temporarily halted further voyages of discovery. Then, in the middle of the 15th century, the entire Middle-East came under Turkish domination, and the once flourishing trade between Europe and the East was cut off. What began as a fanatical dedication to Christendom, became a necessity for economic survival.

Fresh expeditionary fleets were sent out under selected commanders. Among the first was Diego Cão, a man of humble birth but exceptional ability, who reached the mouth of the Congo River in 1483. On his second voyage three years later he stepped ashore on the barren, wind-swept coast of the Kaokoveld, to become the first European to set foot on South West African soil. Here, at present-day Cape Cross, he erected a *padrão,* or limestone cross, which was taken to Germany in 1893 and is now in East Berlin. Today, an inscribed replica in black granite marks this spot where he landed almost 500 years ago.

In 1488 Bartholomew Diaz rounded the Cape and prepared the way for his compatriot Vasco da Gama to reach India ten years later. European settlements in southern Africa followed at the rate of one a century. After a series of bloody wars against the Arabs the Portuguese established themselves in the old island

Bergdamara

Herero

city of Moçambique; in the 16th century they settled in what is today Angola; and a century later the Cape became a victualling station for Dutch ships on their long voyages to and from 'Hinter India', and for the first time the European became a definite force on the African subcontinent.

The inhospitable South West African coast had little to offer passing ships. Seafarers shunned its treacherous seas, and its hinterland and peoples remained a mystery locked behind the waterless wastes of the Namib Desert.

In recent history South West Africa has been inhabited by a great diversity of peoples, of whom only the Bushmen are believed to have roamed its boundless plains in prehistoric times. They were nomads who lived by hunting game and gathering the wild fruits of the veld, unhampered by a culture that valued material wealth. In time they were driven out by successive waves of newcomers to sparser regions. Here their nomadic ways and an intimate knowledge of nature in all its adversity has become crucial to their continued existence.

The well-watered north-eastern region was the home of the Owambo, Kavango and Caprivians. These tribes, all of negroid origin, were settled on the land as cultivators and herders. They had little contact with the migrant war-like tribes of the central and southern areas and largely escaped the turmoil caused by internecine wars among their southern neighbours.

Between two and three centuries ago the Nama, a migrant Hottentot tribe which inhabited the whole of southern Africa before the advent of the European, moved into the country from the south with their herds of cattle and fat-tailed sheep. In the process they forced the Bushmen to the more desolate areas and also drove out or enslaved the Bergdamara, a tribe of nomadic hunters whose way of life resembled that of the Bushman, and whose origins remain a mystery to this day. They are negroid in appearance and it is thought that they may have come from West Africa.

Then from the lake districts of Central Africa, came the Herero to settle in the inhospitable Kaokoveld in the north-west. Towards the middle of the 18th century they moved south, leaving behind the Himba and Tjimba tribes which became a distinctive group which still inhabits this part of the country.

The southward migration of the Herero and their clash with the Nama plunged the country into large-scale bloodshed and violence for almost five decades.

In the early 1800s five clans of mixed Dutch-Hottentot descent crossed the Orange River and settled among the Nama in the south. Called the Orlams, or 'Smart Guys', they were considerably more sophisticated than their hosts, having learnt the use of fire-arms and European way of life from Dutch colonists at the Cape. Among the Orlams were the Afrikaner and Witbooi clans which were to play a prominent part in South West Africa's strife-torn history.

Nama

Nama

Last to appear on the scene were the Basters, descendants of early Dutch colonists at the Cape. They crossed the Orange River with their Hottentot wives and, after a land deal with Chief Swartbooi of the Nama, settled at Rehoboth under their *kaptein* Hermanus van Wyk in 1870 for an annual rental of one horse. Although rejected by the whites, they are extremely proud of their mixed origin and have developed into an exclusive and tight-knit community which is almost totally Afrikaans-speaking. There is no innuendo in the word 'Baster', which is not translatable into the English 'bastard'.

The drought-stricken North-West Cape served to barricade South West Africa for more than a century after the Dutch settled at the Cape. There had been little penetration beyond the coast and the interior remained isolated. But gradually tales of abundant game on the plains north of the Gariep or Great River (the Orange), and even rumours of gold, filtered south. This led Jacobus Coetsé, Dutch colonist and hunter, to cross the Great River on his own initiative in 1760. He reached what is today Warmbad and learned from the Nama of a cattle-rich black race which inhabited the northern regions. Interest grew. The following year an official expedition reached Keetmanshoop and the first map of Namaland was drawn up by land surveyor Carel Brink.

In time the southern regions, home of the Nama, became known as Namaland, or Great Namaqualand; and the northern regions where the black races lived, Damaraland or Hereroland.

Namaqualand's copper riches and talk of gold in the Transgariep, as South West Africa was called at the time, brought Dutch colonist Willem van Reenen to the present Rehoboth in 1791. Here he made first contact with the Herero and obtained samples of copper, which were mistakenly believed to be gold.

During the 18th century English and American whalers operating off the South West African coast established small settlements at Swakopmund and Walvis Bay. Uneasy about the attention the rich waters along the coast were receiving, the Dutch authorities at the Cape annexed all the principal bays and harbours in 1793 to forestall foreign occupation. Then, soon after the first British occupation of the Cape two years later, the Union Jack was hoisted at various points along the South West African coast, primarily to limit whaling and sealing to British vessels. This period ushered in the beginning of trade: cattle were bartered from tribes in the interior and shipped from Walvis Bay to the settlement at St Helena where Napoleon was shortly to be held captive. Significantly, a small cruiser was commissioned by the British to keep foreign traders out – South West Africa was now regarded as of more than purely maritime value.

Nevertheless, it was mainly the desire to minister to the spiritual needs of the indigenous tribes which led to the opening up of this vast unexplored country.

The earliest missionaries to dwell north of the Orange River were the brothers Albrecht, followed by Heinrich Schmelen, first

The Reverend Carl Hugo Hahn

Maharero, William Kamaherero and Chief Amadamap

to master the Nama tongue. He settled with a number of Orlam Hottentots at Bethanien in 1814. Towards the middle of the 19th century the Rhenish Missionary Society, today known in South West Africa as the Evangelical Lutheran Church, took over much of the missionary work in the country and thenceforth played an increasingly important role in the conversion to Christianity of the indigenous peoples and the instilling of a German influence.

The missionaries, labouring under difficult conditions, exercised a settling influence in a country plagued by lawless bands and intermittent wars. They consistently refused to be drawn into intertribal feuds and were often instrumental in making peace between warring factions. Perhaps the most prominent of such mediators was Hugo Hahn who in 1864 established a mission colony at Otjimbingwe on the famous 'Bay Road' between Windhoek and Walvis Bay. Here the Augustineum, a training school for Herero teachers and evangelists, was established by Hugo Hahn in 1866.

By the end of the 19th century most of the Nama had become Christian. In Hereroland the task of the missionaries was made immensely more difficult by the Herero's inherent suspicion of change and attachment to traditional beliefs.

The mission stations gradually developed into small communities where nomadic tribes were taught to settle and work the land. They also served as points of departure for expeditions by missionaries and explorers to distant parts of the country. In fact,

by about 1865 the areas inhabited by the Nama, Herero and Owambo were quite well known.

Meanwhile, European traders had developed a healthy traffic in cattle, dried meat, ivory and ostrich feathers with the tribes of the interior. Windhoek, home of Jonker Afrikaner, head of one of the Orlam clans, had become the most important trading centre: merchandise, arms and ammunition landed at Walvis Bay were brought here along the Bay Road. But while trade burgeoned, unscrupulous dealers exploited the blacks by bartering liquor and arms for cattle. Indeed, trade in arms and ammunition was to inflame the clashes between the Herero and Nama which dominated South West African history during most of the 19th century.

After leaving the Kaokoveld, the Herero had moved south in search of grazing for their ever-increasing herds. The Nama in their turn pressed north where water and grazing were more plentiful.

In the resultant clash the Red Nation of the Hoachanas, oldest of the Nama tribes and thus named by virtue of their dull red complexions, called upon Jonker Afrikaner for assistance. The Herero were driven from Namaland by Jonker's fire-arms and Afrikaner established himself as the most powerful Orlam chief in the land.

In 1840 his people settled around the springs at Windhoek before moving further north to Okahandja from where they systematically plundered and impoverished the Herero in a reign of

10

From the earliest times transport problems have hampered the development of the hinterland

terror which lasted two decades. In 1850 Jonker Afrikaner had hundreds of Herero treacherously murdered in what became known as the 'Bloodbath of Okahandja', earning for himself the sobriquet 'Napoleon of the South'.

After the death of both the Herero chieftain and Jonker Afrikaner, the successor to the Herero throne, Kamaherero, was no longer prepared to remain a vassal of the Nama. He decided to flout the authority of chief Christiaan Afrikaner who was a weakling.

1863 marked the start of war between the Herero and Nama – a war that plunged the entire country into prolonged turmoil. The Nama were driven from Windhoek and became progressively weaker. The Herero also suffered heavily during the 'Scorpion Campaign' when Kamaherero, certain of victory, sent his warriors south without provisions to deal the Nama what he thought would be a final blow. But the country was in the grips of a severe drought and the enemy had scattered southwards. Kamaherero's starving men were forced to search under rocks for scorpions to eat in the course of their retreat. Ultimately both tribes grew weary of war, and in September 1870 peace was made through the intervention of the missionary Hugo Hahn. The war had taken a heavy toll of the Nama, who never regained their former stature. The Herero, on the other hand, won back their freedom and developed steadily into a powerful nation – until their defeat by the Germans in 1904.

The Peace of Okahandja concluded between the Herero and Nama heralded a period of unprecedented reconstruction and progress. The missionaries, from their network of mission stations, dedicated themselves with renewed energy to the conversion of the blacks. Traders returned and the lucrative barter in cattle for the stock fairs at the Cape was resumed. At Walvis Bay, where the guano islands were being exploited under lease from the Cape Government, a settled community of traders and merchants gradually developed.

It was realized by traders and missionaries alike, however, that the country could never be fully developed without a stable central authority. Without protection the missionaries' work was frequently destroyed. Tribal chiefs, constantly supplied with liquor and arms by unscrupulous traders, settled their debts with stolen cattle, thus sparking off endless raids and counter-raids. As early as 1868 the Rhenish Missionary Society had appealed unsuccessfully to King William of Prussia for protection. Now trading interests in the Transgariep began demanding safeguards from the Cape Government with whom lively, although unofficial, contact had been maintained. Kamaherero of the Herero, Jan Jonker of the Afrikaner clan, the Witboois of Gibeon, and Hermanus van Wyk of the Rehoboth Basters were no strangers to the Cape Government. Their names and those of other tribal chiefs appeared more and more frequently in correspondence and reports submitted to the Cape authorities by missionaries

Jan Jonker Afrikaner and his counsellors

and traders. Indeed, Kamaherero and Jan Jonker, alarmed by the arrival of several Boer immigrants in their areas, joined the traders and missionaries in their appeals to the Cape Government for protection.

The Cape, which had been granted responsible government in 1872, welcomed these requests as an opportunity to extend its influence beyond the Orange River. As a first step, special representative William Coates Palgrave was sent to the Transgariep in 1876 with the permission of the British Government, which controlled the Colony's external affairs. His mission was to obtain written requests for protection from the tribal chiefs. As a hunter, explorer and trader during the 1860s he had come to know the Transgariep and enjoyed the confidence of Kamaherero. Thus he had no difficulty in persuading the Herero chieftain to offer the British Government supreme authority over his country and signed the *Treaty of Okahandja* with him. The Nama, on the other hand, had no desire to place themselves under a foreign power. Although Palgrave's efforts were eventually to come to naught, his reports and fine photographs of many of the South West African peoples and their colourful leaders are a valuable record of the period.

While Palgrave was negotiating in the interior, the Cape Government took the first step towards gaining a foothold in South West Africa. On 6 March 1878 the British flag was hoisted over the Walvis Bay settlement which took in the coastal strip as far north as the Swakop River. Six years later this area of 1 165 km² was incorporated into the Cape Colony.

In the rest of the Transgariep relations between the Herero and Nama, at the best of times laden with suspicion, reached breaking-point. Matters came to a head in August 1880 when the Nama murdered Herero herdsmen at a waterhole near Rehoboth and made off with cattle Kamaherero had specially selected for the funeral feast after his death. In retaliation he ordered his own 'Bloodbath of Okahandja' and the murder of every Nama who was spending the night in or near his village. Windhoek, home of the Nama, was destroyed and Jan Jonker Afrikaner fled to the Gamsberg with his tribe.

Waning interest in the regions north of the Orange River and its own border problems, prevented the Cape Government from intervention. While Cape traders were enriching themselves by supplying the belligerents with arms and ammunition, the British Government would only accept responsibility for the safety of British and German subjects in Walvis Bay.

In this sombre political situation Adolf Lüderitz, Bremen-born tobacco dealer, established his trading station in 1883 at what is today known as Lüderitz Bay. He had a burning ambition to found a German colony on the west coast of Africa, and purchased from the Bethanien Hottentot chief, Joseph Fredericks, the bay of Angra Pequena. To this modest piece of desert land he later added the entire coastal strip from the Orange River to 26° South.

The Rehoboth Basterraad

He then petitioned the German Chancellor, Prince Otto von Bismarck, for protection of his Transgariep possessions.

Bismarck was hardly in a position to refuse the request, particularly in the face of strongly imperialist public opinion in Germany. As a new-comer to world politics, she needed overseas colonies for raw materials, as markets for her rapidly expanding industries – and for international prestige.

On 7 August 1884, after prolonged negotiation with Britain, the German flag was hoisted over Lüderitzland to the roar of a 21 gun salute. Captain von Raven was sent north to annex the remainder of the Transgariep coast; and at Cape Cross, a short distance away from Diego Cão's weather-beaten *padrão,* the gunboat crew erected a wooden notice-board proclaiming this rocky crag German property.

The Cape Government made a last desperate attempt to keep Germany out of South West Africa and thwart her expansion into the hinterland. Without the knowledge or permission of the British Government, two envoys were sent from the Cape to the Transgariep to entrench Cape Government influence. Meanwhile British imperialist enthusiasm was on the wane and, in exchange for German support at the height of the Egyptian crisis, she finally acknowledged German claims to the South West African coast. More important, she recognised the hinterland as a German sphere of influence. The Cape Government was ordered to recall its envoys immediately and the ties between the Transgariep and the Cape were severed for good. This unexpected turn of events gives rise to endless speculation as to what South West African history might have been had not international power politics intervened at this point.

Almost overnight Germany was in possession of an overseas territory four times the size of Great Britain. Bismarck's policy was to establish trading settlements rather than colonies, to be administered and developed by chartered companies backed by private capital. To this end the *Deutsche Kolonialgesellschaft für Südwest-Afrika* was formed in 1885 to take over Lüderitz's financially declining interests. Bismarck intended the company to have sovereign authority over its own possessions and, in course of time, the entire Transgariep so that the German taxpayer would be spared the expense of administering and defending South West Africa. At the same time, Germany would be sure of ample raw materials to feed her growing industries. From the outset, however, it was obvious that the German Imperial Government would have to involve itself more directly in South West African affairs.

In May 1885 the administrative machine was appointed. It consisted of Dr Heinrich Göring, Imperial Commissioner and father of the future Luftwaffe chief under the Nazi regime, his secretary Louis Nels, and police sergeant Hugo von Goldammer. Göring was empowered to conclude *Schutzverträge,* or protection treaties, with the tribal chiefs in order to extend German

William Coates Palgrave

Adolf Lüderitz

authority over the entire territory. Nels was responsible for administrative matters, and von Goldammer as chief of police and prison supervisor was to create his own police force by training black constables.

It is remarkable that there was no provision for an armed force with which to honour promises of protection in a country still ravaged by internecine wars.

From the point of view of the new authorities the internal situation in the colony was far from favourable. Internal unrest brought trade to a virtual standstill and the mismanaged Lüderitz empire was headed for financial disaster. The troublesome Witboois still chose to refuse German protection and were quietly preparing themselves in the Gamsberg for an assault on the Herero. In north-western Hereroland a clash between the Swartboois and the Herero was only averted by last-minute German negotiations.

In August 1885 Hendrik Witbooi, the recalcitrant chief of the Witbooi clan and enemy of both the Herero and Germans, tried to force his way through Hereroland where, in a 'vision' the year before, he had seen a bright light calling him north to the promised land. His plans were foiled when his army was routed by the Herero at the Battle of Osana. Two years later he again attacked the Herero, and Kamaherero now demanded the protection afforded him by German treaty: but with an insignificant force at his disposal, Dr Göring was powerless to help. Previous requests

for troops had been summarily turned down by Chancellor Bismarck who contended that armed intervention was contrary to Imperial colonial policy. Robert Lewis, a friend of the Herero chief and a man strongly opposed to German authority over South West Africa, had no difficulty in persuading Kamaherero to break the German protection treaty.

German authority was not only ineffective but virtually non-existent – to the extent that it was openly mocked by the various tribes. Dr Göring withdrew from the explosive political situation in the interior and took refuge at Walvis Bay, which led to much speculation that Germany might withdraw from the territory. On 15 January 1889 such rumours were quashed when the German Chancellor declared in Berlin that Germany had no intention of withdrawing from South West Africa and would defend her interests at all costs.

Determined to restore German prestige and at last convinced that the young colony could not be governed without some military force, Bismarck agreed to send police to South West Africa. Towards the middle of 1889 the first 21 *Schutztruppe,* or protection troops, landed at Walvis Bay under the command of Captain Curt von François who established himself at Tsaobis on the Bay Road and began checking transport wagons for illegal supplies of arms and liquor. But his force was still too weak to take on Hendrik Witbooi who was once more preparing to attack the Herero.

Meanwhile, Bismarck was dismissed as Chancellor on 30

Hendrik Witbooi

Hendrik Witbooi and Nama captains pose with a German official

March 1890 and replaced by Count von Caprivi, whose colonial policy was more dynamic. First priority was given to fixing the borders. In terms of the Anglo-German agreement of 1 July 1890 the boundaries of the territory had been established where they adjoined British possessions, and six years later the boundaries adjoining Portuguese territory were similarly determined.

While waiting for further reinforcements, von François worked to complete the fort still known as the Alte Feste, at Windhoek where the administration was transferred the following year. He also travelled through the country in an attempt to restore German authority and succeeded in pacifying the Herero and persuading a number of Nama tribes to accept German protection from the depredations of the Witboois.

Hendrik Witbooi, the Nama chief, had ignored all appeals to make peace with the Herero. From his mountain stronghold he systematically raided their cattle posts and kept the country in a state of perpetual unrest. In a sudden change of plan, he chose to conclude an unexpected peace with his traditional enemy, the Herero, and began to incite his new-found allies, Rehoboth Basters and Nama against German authority.

He even called upon the Cape Government for assistance in his struggle against the Germans. The von Caprivi Government decided that the time had finally come to subjugate him by force. Von François had received considerable troop reinforcements during 1893 and took the offensive, but he was unable to draw his

wily opponent into decisive battle and the German-Witbooi conflict degenerated into a guerilla war.

Early in 1894 von François was replaced by Major Theodor Leutwein who soon afterwards attacked Hendrik Witbooi and, after a relentless pursuit from one stronghold to another, the tribe was finally subjugated. Witbooi, one of the most colourful figures in South West African history, was allowed to return with a German pension to his home at Gibeon. Ten years later he was to fall in battle on the farm Witbooisende near Keetmanshoop after he had taken up arms to defend his people's cause for the last time.

Despite internal unrest during the first ten years of German occupation, steady progress was made in all spheres of commerce and industry. Various companies and syndicates were formed to develop the territory's economy. The *Deutsche Kolonialgesellschaft für Südwest-Afrika,* originally the largest land and mining company in the territory, took over Adolf Lüderitz's properties and mining concessions. The *Siedlungsgesellschaft für Deutsch-Südwest-Afrika* undertook the settlement of colonists on small-holdings at Klein Windhoek. In 1895 the *Damara-Guano Kompagnie* obtained a concession to hunt seals and collect guano.

Ever since the time of Adolf Lüderitz prospecting for minerals had continued unabated and a spate of mining concessions was granted. Expeditions were continually sent into the interior, at great expense, in the hope of discovering a new El Dorado.

Captain Curt von François

Adventurers and fortune seekers regularly spread rumours of discoveries which were either non-existent or exaggerated. Six Australian miners in 1887 created a furore by announcing that they had found gold near Otjimbingwe. But, as was so often the case, the facts did not bear out the myth: the ore was of such low quality that the project was soon abandoned.

The South West Africa Company was formed in London with British capital to exploit the copper mines at Tsumeb. In view of the riches there, survey work for the construction of a railway to the coast was begun.

1890 saw the birth of the lucrative sheep-farming industry. The model farms Hoffnung and Unverzagt were laid out near Windhoek to promote farming among young colonists: dams were built and a start made with the breeding of horses, cattle, sheep and angora goats.

Constitutional development up to this stage was insignificant. The system of mercantile self-government under supreme Imperial authority gradually developed into civil government. The foundation was laid in 1894 by Governor Leutwein who established *Bezirksämter,* or district offices, at Windhoek and Keetmanshoop. Sections of the *Schutztruppe* were transferred to the civil administration as police, and courts were set up in major towns.

Harsh conditions in the new colony and intermittent unrest among the indigenous peoples undoubtedly retarded immigration. But, despite this, the white population continued to grow.

Colonists were brought out from Germany and frequent attempts were made to settle ex-soldiers as farmers. Since the earliest times immigrants of Dutch stock had entered the country as hunters, traders or transport-riders. Now, after the German occupation, Boer families, either individually or in groups, crossed the Orange River to settle on land bartered from the Nama. By 1896 more than 700 Boers were living in South West Africa: indeed it was only the fear that the territory would lose its German character that subsequently brought an end to large-scale Boer immigration. Nevertheless, by 1910 there were over 10 000 whites living in South West Africa.

This decade of relatively peaceful growth came to a sudden end on 25 October 1903, when the Bondelswarts of Warmbad, one of the many indigenous tribes, killed their district officer. The uprising was quickly suppressed by Governor Leutwein: but a more serious rebellion was building up in Hereroland.

Discontent and suspicion of the Germans and their foreign customs had been smouldering for a long time among the Herero. Added to this was ill-feeling over the alienation of tribal land and cattle in favour of colonists and white creditors. Now, with the *Schutztruppe* concentrated in the south to quell the Nama uprising, the Herero saw their chance.

The rebellion broke out in the second week of January 1904. On Kamaherero's personal orders English and Boer settlers, missionaries, women and children were spared; but more than

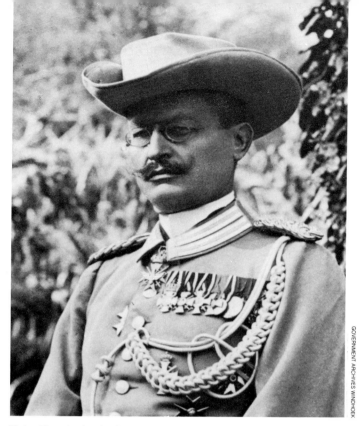

Major Theodor Leutwein

General Lothar von Trotha

100 Germans were surprised and killed. In the ensuing conflict the railway between Windhoek and Swakopmund was destroyed in several places and telegraph communications were disrupted. The white population took refuge in the local town forts where they were besieged by the Herero. After they had been systematically relieved by the *Schutztruppe,* the main force of the Herero was drawn into battle at Oviumbo and defeated. Thereupon the entire Herero tribe withdrew to the Waterberg in the north to await the German troops for the final confrontation.

The murder of German citizens hardened the German authorities who no longer found Leutwein's conciliatory policies towards the indigenous peoples of South West Africa acceptable. Early in 1904 he was replaced by General Lothar von Trotha, who had personal instructions from the German Kaiser, Wilhelm II, to suppress the Herero insurrection with every means at his disposal.

On 11 August 1904, under a blistering sun, the Herero were encircled and defeated in bloody battle. Some of the surviving tribesmen succeeded in breaking out of the encirclement during the night. Thousands of human and animal lives were lost on the arduous journey through the waterless wastes of the Omaheke sandveld in an attempt to reach the safety of present-day Botswana. Others fled into the bush and were hunted down by German troops.

While the *Schutztruppe* were still engaged in the Herero campaign, Jacob Morenga of the Bondelswarts and his armed men began to foment fresh rebellion in parts of Namaland. They were joined by the Fransman Hottentots, the Red Nation and the Veldskoendraers. Even Hendrik Witbooi fell under their influence and took up arms against the German authorities.

It took two years to suppress the rebellion which left the Nama reduced to a few hundred fighting men and saw the supreme command of the German General Staff change six times.

The revolts exacted a heavy toll on all sides. The Germans suffered over 2 000 casualties and had to foot a war bill of 600 million marks. When the armistice was signed on 20 December 1905 only some 16 000 Herero remained from an original population of between 60 000 and 80 000. Between 75% and 80% of the population had perished in the war which, for them, lasted a year. Three years of guerilla war had cost the Nama between 35% and 50% of their people, many of whom died in the notorious prisoner-of-war camp on Shark Island. The Nama and Herero lost all their cattle; they lost their land and their tribal organisations were dissolved: but one of the most unfortunate effects of the war was that the Herero lost their traditional customs and identity.

In 1908 the last serious rebellion, led by the Nama chief Simon Koper, was put down and the country at last entered a period of long-desired peace, marked by lively economic development and increased self-government.

On 19 June 1902 the first passenger train arrived at Wind-

Girls at Afrikaner's kraal

hoek after a four-day journey over the newly-constructed line between Swakopmund and the capital; in time railways were to join many of the major towns and mining areas. As early as 1901 the territory was linked by telegraph with Germany, and two years later the new pier at Swakopmund provided it with a second important harbour.

Perhaps the most significant event in South West African history occurred in 1908 when diamonds were discovered near Lüderitz Bay. Fortune-seekers streamed in by sea and land. A multitude of companies sprang up, some of them paying a return of over 3 000% on invested capital. Lüderitz Bay mushroomed into a boom town, reminiscent of Kimberley in the Cape during the diamond rush of the 1870s. Overnight the territory won financial independence and could provide employment for blacks divorced from their traditional existence after the Herero and Nama rebellions. Since that day 70 years ago when Zacharia Lewala found the first gemstone a few kilometres from Lüderitz Bay, the South West African diamond industry has become a giant concern which extracts stones to the value of R100 million annually from the wind-swept sands of the Namib Desert.

In 1907 the first karakul sheep, forerunners of the breed used for today's booming karakul pelt industry, were imported from Germany.

Just as German possession of South West Africa in the first place had been decided in Europe, so was her loss of this colony the result of events far from Southern Africa. The outbreak of World War I in August 1914 ushered in the final phase of German rule in South West.

The Union of South Africa was allied with Britain against Germany and accepted responsibility for the conquest of German South West Africa. After putting down some Afrikaner opposition to South African support for Britain, Prime Minister Louis Botha assumed personal command of the Union forces for a three-pronged invasion of South West.

The battle plan was for General MacKenzie to advance from Lüderitz Bay, and General Lukin to cross the Orange River at Ramansdrif; and on Christmas Day 1914, South African troops landed at Walvis Bay. Colonel van Deventer advanced with 5 000 mounted soldiers along a specially constructed railway line in the Cape Colony to the south-western corner of the territory, and Swakopmund was bombarded from the sea.

The Union forces consisted of some 40 000 well-equipped and well-trained men: the Germans could muster only 2 000 regulars, supported by some 7 000 reservists. The odds against the Germans were made even less favourable by new methods of warfare employed by the Union forces. Armoured motorized vehicles made their first appearance and the South West African campaign saw another innovation in the use of aeroplanes for military reconnaissance.

Against such heavy odds all the Germans could do was

Camel transport during the 1914 campaign

employ delaying tactics in the hope of an early German victory in Europe. By a series of outflanking movements, carried out at great speed, they were steadily driven further inland. At Karibib unsuccessful truce talks were held between General Botha and Dr Theodor Seitz, the Imperial Governor.

Continuing their successful occupation of the territory, on 11 May 1915 General Botha entered Windhoek with his forces.

Meanwhile Dr Seitz had moved his government to the well-watered Waterberg region in the north where all the German troops were concentrated and entrenched. The German commander was confident that the Union forces would be unable to cross the almost waterless wastes in between with their horses, wagons and troops. Here a bold plan was devised by the German command to link up with General Lettow von Vorbeck's forces in East Africa, but it was thwarted by General Brits moving in from the north-east. To the surprise of the Germans, the Union forces had negotiated the desert regions by using a thousand lorries to transport water. Further resistance was useless. To prevent war matériel from falling into the hands of the enemy the Germans dumped large quantities of munitions into lake Otjikoto near Tsumeb, and on 9 July 1915 capitulated near the town of Otavi.

With the signing of the *Peace of Khorab* the German Flag, which had flown for 31 eventful years, was lowered over South West Africa for the last time.

But for international practice which allows the annexation of conquered territory only at the end of hostilities, the South African Prime Minister Louis Botha, supported by the Imperial War Cabinet, would probably have annexed South West Africa after its occupation by Union forces in 1915. As it was, the German civil administration had been immediately replaced by an interim South African military government, superseded in the same year by an administrator.

In terms of the *Treaty of Versailles* of 1919 Germany surrendered all her colonies to the Allied Powers. But when it came to deciding what should be done with them differences of opinion became immediately apparent. South Africa, together with certain other countries, favoured outright annexation by the occupying states. However, other voices were to prevail. President Woodrow Wilson of the United States of America was adamant: he wanted full authority and control vested in the newly-founded League of Nations.

The deadlock was finally resolved by the mandate system whereby the administering states acted as mandators on behalf of the League of Nations. This compromise agreement placed former German colonies 'inhabited by peoples not yet able to stand by themselves' under the guidance of more advanced nations. The agreement signed in Geneva in December 1920 entrusted South West Africa to South Africa as a 'C' class mandate in terms of which it was to be administered as an integral part of the Union. She was required to promote the material and moral

General Louis Botha leaves the Rathaus in Windhoek after the capitulation of the city in May 1915

well-being of the territory's inhabitants and submit annual reports to the nine-member Permanent Mandates Commission of the League of Nations.

From the outset the Commission and South Africa disagreed as to the exact interpretation of the South West African mandate. In 1925 their divergent views were accentuated when South Africa granted South West representative government. A partly-elected Legislative Assembly was established which led to the formation of political parties, each with its own very definite views on the political future of the country. At one extreme, a branch of the German Nazi Party in Windhoek agitated for South West Africa's return to Germany; on the other, the United National South West Party, a zealous champion of incorporation during the thirties, repeatedly requested the Union Government to incorporate South West as a fifth province of South Africa.

Initially the Permanent Mandates Commission displayed little interest in the administration of South West Africa. The Union was largely left to deal with matters as it saw fit. But from 1926 the Commission began to show increasing interest in the indigenous peoples of the territory, partly because it was alarmed by the repeated appeals for incorporation of South West Africa with the Union, and also perhaps in response to a world-wide trend towards humanism. The Commission now began to criticise the Union Government's annual reports on the grounds that the indigenous peoples were being discriminated against socially

and politically. Furthermore it demanded to know what her intentions were with regard to incorporation. Basically, the Union Government saw no real difference between the 'C' mandate and annexation: indeed in her view, South West Africa could be annexed as a fifth province and granted representation in the Union Parliament.

The Commission found this proposal totally unacceptable. However, the outbreak of World War II shifted attention to more urgent matters and the South West African issue was left unresolved.

After World War II, in 1945, the conflicting viewpoints between South Africa and the now defunct League of Nations were soon echoed in the new United Nations Organization. It proposed that South Africa should enter into a trusteeship agreement with the world body, placing South West Africa under the supervision of its Trusteeship Council – a request which was rejected by South Africa on the grounds that the mandate over South West Africa had expired with the demise of the League of Nations and that South Africa did not recognise the new world body as the legal successor. South African Prime Minister Jan Smuts, esteemed world-statesman, thereupon requested permission from the United Nations Organization to annex the territory formally. This claim was rejected by the world body. In time the dispute reached an impasse, the salient features of which have remained the same to this day. Although it has been put forward

Herero and Kung Bushmen

for arbitration, the argument continues to go back and forth from one forum to another without as yet finding a solution acceptable to all concerned.

In 1948 the South African United Party, led by Field-Marshal Smuts, was defeated at the polls in a general election. This brought about far-reaching changes in South Africa and affected policy governing South West Africa as well. Dr D.F. Malan's National Party, like its predecessor, not only denied any supervisory powers the United Nations claimed it had over South West Africa, but even refused to submit further reports or transmit petitions from the inhabitants of the territory.

On a political level, South Africa's administration of South West Africa was at this stage characterised by a striving for a greater measure of self-government and closer constitutional links with the territory.

After repeated debate in the United Nations the South West Africa dispute entered the international law court for the first time. In 1949 the General Assembly asked the International Court of Justice for an advisory opinion on the status of the territory. The court ruled unanimously that South Africa was under no obligation to conclude a trusteeship agreement with the United Nations Organization, but made it quite clear that South Africa could not alter the status of the territory unilaterally. South Africa repudiated the decision and the impasse deepened.

Political and diplomatic battle raged throughout the fifties with various proposals and counter-proposals coming from the interested parties. The result was that the United Nations' repeated appeals that South West Africa be placed under trusteeship were ignored by South Africa who in her turn continued to administer the territory according to the mandate entrusted to her.

The next serious attempt to end the deadlock occurred in 1959 when serious rioting, in which a number of blacks lost their lives, broke out in Windhoek. Angry black African states, which were already becoming a powerful force in international politics, instituted legal proceedings against South Africa. In the same year, the issue was taken for arbitration to the International Court of Justice at The Hague.

The plaintiffs were Ethiopia and Liberia – the only independent African states which had been members of the former League of Nations.

Officially the charge was a breach of South Africa's obligations under the mandate entrusted to her. Unofficially it amounted to the Court's being asked to rule that the policy of *apartheid* was against the best interests of the territory's black inhabitants. The findings of the International Court of Justice would be legally binding and enforceable by the Security Council, most powerful organ of the United Nations. A legal battle of amazing complexity followed.

While the case was being argued, the dispute found its way

Councillors from Kavango

back to the political arena. The General Assembly, in 1960, instructed the Committee on South West Africa to investigate the question of a greater measure of self-government for the indigenous peoples of the territory. The South African Government refused to allow the United Nations Committee into South West Africa. As an alternative, it suggested that the territory be visited by a person of international standing who could carry out an impartial and objective investigation to determine whether or not peace and security were being threatened by South Africa's administration of South West Africa.

This led to the hapless visit, in 1962, of a two-man special committee under the chairmanship of Vittorio Carpio of the Philippines. In a joint communiqué it was declared that South West Africa did not pose a threat to world peace and that no signs of either militarism or the extermination of the indigenous people could be found.

A report-back memorandum to the world body repudiated the findings of the Special Committee and recommended that the United Nations itself take over the administration of South West Africa.

In 1966, after five years of involved legal dispute, the International Court of Justice, by the casting vote of its President, Sir Percy Spender, dismissed the Ethiopian and Liberian application on the grounds that they were not competent to lay a charge against South Africa. The judgement came as a blow to those who wanted to see the ties between South West Africa and South Africa severed.

In South Africa the judgement was hailed as a victory. But at best it was a technical one in that the United Nations was thwarted in its attempt to obtain an enforceable judgement on South West Africa. The dispute had now been waged for almost half a century and the real issues were never judged by the World Court and remained unresolved.

A frustrated United Nations reacted by adopting Resolution 2145, in terms of which South Africa's mandate over South West Africa was terminated. An 11-nation Council for South West Africa was established to administer the territory in exile and the country was renamed 'Namibia'.

Meanwhile South Africa continued to invest vast sums of money in South West Africa to develop the country, mainly in a hydro-electric project on the Kunene River, water schemes and roads. The Government of the Republic of South Africa at the same time increasingly applied its policy of separate development to South West Africa by implementing the proposals of the Odendaal Commission, which recommended the establishment of a stable and inalienable homeland for each of the ten non-white population groups. Politically, it was intended that the indigenous peoples would be guided towards South African-style self-governing homelands.

This proposed fragmentation of the territory met with uncom-

Delegates at the 1976 constitutional talks in Windhoek

promising opposition from the United Nations and African states that wanted to preserve South West Africa as an entity. International pressure on South Africa mounted. And, on 12 August 1969 the Security Council, for the first time, passed a resolution setting a date by which South Africa had to withdraw its administration from South West Africa. In June 1971 this was given added force by a ruling of the International Court of Justice that South Africa end what it termed its 'illegal' administration of the country.

However, the dates determined for South African withdrawal from the territory have since been repeatedly postponed because of the world body's inability to enforce its decisions.

In 1972 the nature of the dispute changed significantly when it was decided to re-open negotiations with South Africa. The Security Council gave its Secretary-General, Dr Kurt Waldheim, a mandate 'to initiate contacts with all the parties concerned to establish conditions under which the inhabitants of Namibia could exercise their right to self-determination and independence'. Visits by Dr Waldheim and his personal representative in the same year elicited assurances from the South African Government that its policy for the territory was now moving in this direction. In fact, in 1973 South African Prime Minister B. J. Vorster declared that the inhabitants of South West Africa should themselves decide on the political future of their country.

Meanwhile public appeals both in South Africa and South West Africa urged the speeding-up of a solution to the dispute.

Subsequently the territory's Legislative Assembly passed a resolution in August 1974 for constitutional talks between representatives of the various population groups to try and achieve a consensus on the future of South West Africa.

A year later, in September 1975, delegates representing all the peoples of South West Africa convened in the historic Turnhalle in Windhoek. A Declaration of Intent was issued committing the conference to a new constitution for the territory, the promotion of human rights irrespective of race or colour, and the safe-guarding of minority rights. In the spirit of the declaration, discriminatory laws are now being abolished.

The inhabitants of South West Africa are greatly divided on the constitutional future of the country. The general attitude among the white population is that change is essential. But, like other minority groups, they are unlikely to accept a settlement which does not guarantee their rights. Even the indigenous peoples are divided. The traditional chiefs of the north appear to favour a policy that ensures the independence of each homeland as a separate entity. Others, like the South West Africa People's Organisation (SWAPO), want a unitary independent South West Africa.

After years of uncertainty and dispute South West Africans, in spite of these differences, are for the first time acting together to find a common destiny for their land.

1

1 A Namib dune, sculpted by chill sea winds and wreathed in mist. In the mid-19th century Charles Andersson, an early explorer of South West Africa (the name he gave to what had until then been known as the Transgariep), wrote of the Namib Desert : '. . . a place fitter to represent the infernal regions could scarcely, in searching the world around, be found. A shudder, amounting almost to fear, came over me when its frightful desolation first broke upon my view. Death, I exclaimed, would be preferable to banishment in such a country.'

2

3

4

5

Diamonds and South West are synonymous. North of the Orange River mouth for a distance of 100 kilometres along the desert coast lies the world's greatest single deposit of gem diamonds. They are found in gravels on marine terraces now raised above sea-level and buried under thousands of tons of sand. To reach these hidden riches, open bowl-scrapers must remove a staggering amount of overburden to reveal the gravel and bedrock.

2 As much gravel as possible is first removed by hydraulic excavators. Then the bedrock is scoured by hand, brushes and prying fingers extracting every last grain of gravel. **3** Some of the 4 500 Owambo workers employed by the diamond mines. **4** A view from the wall of a 'paddock'. It was only in the 1960s that diamonds were first extracted from the shoreline, the methods used representing a triumph of engineering and technical skill. In order to mine the upper half of the beaches the overburden is bulldozed into coffer dams to hold back the sea. Heavy excavators then scoop away the remaining sand until the gravel is reached, often many metres below sea-level. **5** Every crevice of this pitted bedrock will be scoured for hidden treasure. **6** An open bowl-scraper, assisted by two bulldozers, clears the overburden before mining can begin.

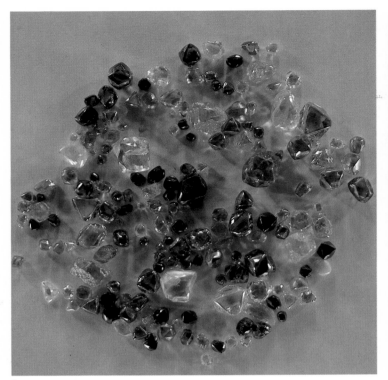

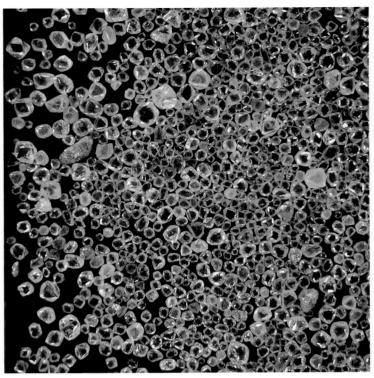

7 8 9

7 Each gem unique, this priceless collection shows diamonds of every shade. Carat weight, colour, clarity and cut determine the value, but the rarity of pure coloured stones such as these, places them in a class of their own. Incredibly, approximately 90% of the diamonds found at Oranjemund are of gem quality, but where they came from is uncertain. Some believe that they originated far inland, perhaps from kimberlite pipes at places like Orapa, Finsch and Kimberley, and were swept by the Orange River and ancient flood waters down to the sea. Here the gems were carried by currents along the coast before waves flung them back on to the beaches which were themselves in time raised, creating the diamond-rich marine terraces. Others claim that there are as yet undiscovered diamondiferous pipes beneath the sea and that the gems are washed up from the ocean bed. Whichever the case, they have been buffeted by the sea and it is even possible that this inexorable action may account for their superb quality. **8** A single day's production at the recovery plant at Oranjemund. **9** A treatment plant belonging to the Consolidated Diamond Mines of South West Africa (Pty) Ltd – more commonly known as CDM – at Oranjemund. CDM, a member of the De Beers Group, was formed by the late Sir Ernest Oppenheimer in 1920, thereby merging the interests of several companies that had until then separately mined diamonds in the territory. Today it is a vast organisation with headquarters at Oranjemund, its annual production amounting to some one and a half million carats. The entire coastal area from the north bank of the Orange River in the southernmost part of South West Africa to a point approximately 80 kilometres north of Lüderitz has been proclaimed a prohibited area – the Sperrgebiet.

10

11

12

13

14

10 A ghost town at Elizabeth Bay stands as silent testimony to the activities of early diamond hunters. The history of diamonds in South West Africa dates back to 1908 when August Stauch, a young railway supervisor, told his labourers to watch out for pretty stones. Scarcely two weeks had passed before Zacharias Lewala, a coloured man who had worked at Kimberley, discovered the first diamond. The rush was soon on. Thousands converged on the Sperrgebiet to make their fortunes, and towns sprang up near the new finds. World War I temporarily halted mining and when, in the late twenties, the industry revived it was the newly discovered marine terraces of the south that became the centre of activity. Here the industry was to develop into the giant it is today. As for the mining areas in the northern part of the Sperrgebiet, they progressively faded from importance. **11 12 13** Kolmanskop, where the first diamonds were found, is now an empty shell, smothered by relentless shifting sand. **14** The Namib Desert's dreaded coast. Ceaselessly, sand is washed ashore and the beaches widen so that wrecks eventually lie far from the sea, buried in the sands and then exposed by shifting dunes and storms.

15

16

17

15 Salvaged soon after World War II and now discarded, this converted tank was used to remove overburden in the Sperrgebiet. **16** Against a misty background, a grader prepares a road in the desert. The Namib is shielded from the searing summer heat by cool sea mists that drift daily inland for part of the year. **17** The Bogenfels (literally, *bogen* meaning 'bow' and *fels* 'rock'), a dramatic formation on the Sperrgebiet coast. Dolomite, over 600 million years old, is ceaselessly battered by violent seas, the more resistant top layers bravely withstanding erosion to form the arch. If the sea would allow, a small freighter could safely pass through the 60 metre-high arch.

18

19

20

18 A Cape Fur Seal cow comes ponderously ashore. The delightful pups gambol at the water's edge while their mothers hunt for food out at sea. This species, endemic to southern Africa, is the largest of all fur seals and some 70 000 yearlings are clubbed to death annually for the sake of their valuable pelts. Yet, despite this, the colonies on South West Africa's coast continue to grow – the largest seal colony in Africa, Atlas Bay, has a breeding population of 180 000! That it thrives is probably due to undisturbed breeding along the Sperrgebiet coast and the fact that, besides the Black-backed Jackal and Strandwolf, the Cape Fur Seal has few natural enemies on land. Culling is strictly controlled. **19** A dingy scrap of fisherman's net makes a nest for these Cape Cormorants breeding on one of South West's many tiny offshore islands. In 1828 an American sealer, Captain Morrell, discovered that the immense breeding colonies of gannets, cormorants and penguins had deposited a layer of veritable 'white gold' on these islands. Guano, that pungent nitrate-rich fertilizer, lay up to 20 metres deep in places and soon became the focus of the 'Great Guano Rush'. Opportunists and entrepreneurs battled furiously for a chance to load their ships. Rarely has a natural legacy been more relentlessly over-exploited and now, less than 150 years later, only the vestiges of the once-thriving guano industry remain. **20** Cows, pups and a lone bull (far right) crowd the breeding colony at Atlas Bay. During October the dominant males, their massive bodies bloated with stored fat, come on land and noisily proclaim their territories. Shortly afterwards the cows, each heavy with pup, come ashore to breed and quickly sort themselves out under the protection of a bull, which may acquire up to 60 females in his harem. Then, within a month, almost all the pups are born – yet Nature wastes no time in restarting the cycle. A mere week after giving birth the females come on heat and copulate with their masters – plus an occasional lucky young bull without territory but keen all the same. A year later, almost to the day, the entire scene will be re-enacted. As for the newborn pups – those that survive disease, the attacks of jackal, or being squashed by eager bulls during the mating period – they remain in the vicinity of the colony with their mothers until the following breeding season when they are sent off to fend for themselves. Meanwhile the bulls, accompanied by the sub-adults, swim far out to sea to feed, living entirely in the water and building up a good reserve of fat for the end-of-year festivities ashore.

21

22

23

21 A tapestry of pinks and orange, the mighty Koichab plains just north of Lüderitz. **22** In the barren wastelands of the Namib, the ostrich lives. Standing 2,5 metres when fully grown, it grazes on succulent roots and grasses, drawing much of its liquid requirements from the sap and dew licked from grass stems in the early morning. Ferocious when provoked, these birds have been known to disembowel a man with vicious blows from their two-toed feet. Probably the best form of defence is either to brandish a stick at the ostrich's head or hide in a thorn bush which the bird will not approach for fear of damaging its large vulnerable eyes on which it depends for seeking food. **23** Gnarled acacias seem to clutch at the earth for their tenuous existence on the fringe of the Namib. The truffle, beloved by gourmets everywhere, often hides among the acacia's roots, just as it does beneath the oak tree in Europe. **24** Carved by a restless wind, these stark Namib dunes are home to a surprising host of small creatures. Over many millenia a life has evolved adapted to the uncompromising harshness of the shifting sands. Drawing moisture from the dense fog that daily hangs over the Namib, and feeding on the wind-borne organic detritus that tumbles from windswept slope to lee, the creatures of the desert survive and multiply.

25

26

27

28

25 By crawling up the trunks of trees, these snails catch cooling breezes and find respite from the tropical sun. Inadvertently imported from Europe with horse fodder during the Anglo-Boer War (1899 – 1902), the *Theba pisana* has adapted well to its African home. **26** As if painted on pitted rock by some Bushman artist, a gemsbok flees across the rippled landscape. Under the harsh sun the gemsbok's great body absorbs an enormous amount of heat – so much so that the blood temperature rises to levels that would normally destroy an animal's brain. Many mammals in the desert share the gemsbok's ability to store heat in its body during the day and gradually dissipate it during the night; but in a further incredible adaptation to its environment, the blood of the gemsbok's brain first circulates through a fine network of blood vessels in the nose to cool. **27** The coast near Lüderitz. **28** After the heaviest rains for 30 years, the landscape round Naute Dam, south-west of Keetmanshoop, luxuriates under a mantle of fresh new growth.

29

30

31

32

29 Few parts of South West Africa enjoy adequate surface water; indeed over most of the country windmills endlessly tap the vast underground reservoirs in which Nature has trapped this precious liquid. **30** Karakul sheep grazing on the arid southern plains. 'Swakara' is a magic word to women who dream of revelling in the silken pelts of newborn karakul lambs. To meet ever-increasing world-wide demand, almost 3,5 million pelts are exported annually. **31** North and central South West is cattle country, although the carrying capacity of the land is low and ranches are inversely vast. Despite the erratic and none-too-plentiful rainfall, ranching is the main money-spinner in terms of agriculture and over 3 million head are raised, largely for export. **32** Typical of the south are sheep which appear to flourish on the coarse scrub. **33** Worn-down spades symbolize this farmer's struggle to coax his unyielding land into fruitfulness.

34 One of the oldest breeds of domesticated sheep is the karakul, said to have originated in central Asia from where it reached South West Africa via Germany in 1907. At birth the karakul lamb's pelt is smooth and dark, marked with the finely variegated wavelets of curls for which it is so admired. **35** Sunset over the Pro-Namib, the stark semi-desert region that lies between the desolate coast and the highlands.

36

37

38

39

40

36 Bougainvilia spills over a wall beside this quaint old house in Mariental. **37** Country parents see their children off to boarding-school. Most youngsters receive their education far from home because distances between towns are immense and the rural population is thinly scattered. **38** Unintended humour, a sign outside a country general-dealer's store delivers its message in a garbled mixture of English and Afrikaans. **39** A German bakery in the proud European tradition. **40** Rehoboth, home since 1870 of the Rehoboth Basters who originally settled here under their *kaptein* Hermanus van Wyk. 'A state within a state', this area, now known as the Rehoboth Gebiet, was obtained from the Swartboois for the annual rental of one horse. Today's 19 000 Basters are descended from early Dutch colonists at the Cape who travelled north beyond the Orange River with their Hottentot wives where they have developed into an exclusive, tightly-knit community. Law-abiding citizens, they still look for patriarchal authority to their *kaptein* and *kaptein's* council.

41

42

43

44

41 Popular with watersport enthusiasts and fresh-water fishermen, the Hardap Dam provides superb recreation while at the same time marshalling the erratic flow of the Fish River. **42** A ribbon of dusty white road crosses endless miles of dull red Kalahari sand, the scrub and occasional tree barely breaking the monotony. **43** Running from here to infinity, or so it seems, a railway line near Grünau in the south. **44** '*Mukurob*', the Hottentot word for the 'Finger of God', an amazing 34 metre-high column of eroded schist south of Gibeon.
45 Beautiful in its desolation, spell-binding in its silence, the Fish River coils sluggishly round and round like the rings of a python. The mud-curdled waters flow fitfully, often dwindling to nothing, and finally join the mighty Orange River on its way to the sea. Worn down by surging flood-waters from a wetter age long past, the canyon's jutting buttresses guard deep pools of precious water for the zebra, buck, baboons and other hardy creatures that make this their home. Within the confining canyon walls temperatures rise to 45°C during the day, and hot sulphurous springs bubble up from the floor. At Ai-Ais people seek miracle cures from the hot springs known as the 'Lourdes of South West'.

46

47

48   49

The peoples of the south are quite distinctive, particularly those of Hottentot stock. Where today's 37 000 Nama came from is a mystery, but their physical characteristics leave no doubt as to their origins. They are descendants of the Xhoi-Xhoi, the 'men of men', who share the Bushman's linguistic clicks and mongoloid eyes, peppercorn hair, bridgeless nose and yellow skin. But their culture immediately sets them apart from the diminutive desert hunters. The Nama are herders who were already well-established in the southern part of South West Africa by the 17th century. Divided into eight clans, which carry such evocative names as the Bondelswarts, Veldskoendraers, the Red Nation of the Hoachanas, the Topnaars and the Great Dead, their numbers were later strengthened by the infusion of five Orlam tribes from the Cape. Among them were the Afrikaners and Witboois whose names were to recur constantly in South West Africa's strife-torn history. Today the Nama still practise stockfarming, although some have left to work on white-owned farms or in the small towns of the south.

46 Staring stolidly at the camera, this stock-farmer's weather-beaten yellow skin proclaims his proud Nama heritage.   **47** Taking a break, a Baster couple drink tea in the yard of their house.   **48** A delicate heart-shaped face and warm honey-toned skin reflect this young Nama girl's Hottentot blood.   **49** Against a backdrop of angry storm clouds, a Nama family travels by donkey-cart through the parched landscape.

50

51

50 Not for decades has rain fallen like this in the Namib, which is lucky to receive 25 mm a year in normal times. **51** The Fish River in expansive mood, its middle-course near Seeheim flooded by the recent rains. **52** Some of the highest sand dunes in the world (up to 300 metres) crowd Sossusvlei, a level clay pan hidden deep in the Namib. Here live gemsbok and other game, totally dependent on the vlei for water and the life-giving vegetation that taps its underground moisture. Rarely does the Tsauchab River feed the vlei, more usually small watercourses and underground flows replenish the supply.

53

54

53 Relentlessly driven forward by the wind, this dune looms threateningly over a group of trees near Sossusvlei. In time it will engulf them in its soft yellow belly, and eventually, when it moves on, the desiccated and lifeless trunks will appear once more. **54** Towering dunes create parabolas of shade and light. The Namib, oldest unchanged desert in the world, has over aeons evolved a unique fauna. Condensation from the night-fogs provides some 40 mm of moisture annually and a host of highly adapted creatures make almost miraculous use of this source of liquid. Others, without this ability to drink from the air, feed on the creatures that do so, and prosper. Whereas moisture comes from the west, food is brought by the hot east winds. Plant detritus and miniscule particles of organic matter sweep over the dunes, much of it collecting in the troughs between and remaining there as a 'larder' on which the desert creatures can draw. Surprisingly, the dunes cast a great deal of shade and this, combined with the cooling effect of the sea mists, has led to a further specialization of fauna. There are the 'crawlers' that scamper swiftly over the compacted surface of the seaward slopes, and there are the 'creepers' that move softly over the yielding sands of the slip-face; there are those that revel in the sun, and those that venture out only at night; there are the surface dwellers and those that burrow into the cooler depths of the sand to hide from the sun. Each is unique, and scientists drawn from every corner of the globe come to marvel at and study this living desert.

55

56

57

58

59

55 Windhoek, capital of South West Africa, has had a history as diverse as its names. The Herero called it Otjomuise (the place of smoke) and the original Hottentot name for it was Ai-gams after the hot springs around which tribes settled in early times. Captain James Alexander gave it its first European name in 1837 when he called it Queen Adelaide's Bath after the then queen of England. In 1842 it was called Elbersfeld by the missionaries Hahn and Kleinschmidt before the Wesleyan mission changed it to Concordiaville in 1844. The name Windhoek was first used by Jonker Afrikaner – probably a corruption of Winterhoek because the surrounding mountains reminded him of the farm near Tulbagh in the Cape from which he emigrated to South West Africa. However, the indigenous tribes referred to it rather pointedly as 'The Place of the Sheep-stealers' after Jonker and his Afrikaner tribe had settled there. Windhoek was for many years the battle-ground of warring tribes and

changed hands as often as it was destroyed. After Jonker's defeat at the hands of the Herero, Windhoek was a no-man's land until, in 1890, Curt von François, with his men, built the Alte Feste and thereby founded the town. Since then the population has grown steadily and Windhoek has developed into a modern city alive with 20th century activity. Here, the atmosphere of Europe mingles with the mood of Africa and gives Windhoek its particular cosmopolitan air.
56 Kaiserstrasse, Windhoek's main thoroughfare. **57** Herero men, always fussy dressers, spend lavishly on clothing and can be counted on to add colour and style to Windhoek's streets. **58** Another ingredient in Windhoek's heterogeneous mixture of peoples and cultures, Nama girls watch the passing crowds. Their bright scarves barely conceal the dozens of hair-rollers that are almost standard head-gear for many coloured women. **59** Gleaming escalators in a modern Windhoek shopping centre.

60

61

62

63

60 One of Windhoek's many beer-gardens where people meet to talk over tankards of the excellent brew. **61** *Gemütlichkeit* and foaming steins of beer draw regulars to this pub in Swakopmund. **62** The Daan Viljoen Game Park, near Windhoek, lies in the picturesque Khomas Hochland. Cool gardens harbour approximately 200 species of birds and provide a welcome escape from the wild countryside that surrounds the capital. **63** Wild-life safaris attract tourists, but licences to shoot are issued with care and conservation is the watch-word. **64** Jacarandas cast a gentle canopy over a Tsumeb street. Often called 'the garden city of South West' it is ironical that ever-thirsty South West has apparently vast water-supplies deep underground. Thanks to the thriving mining industry, millions of litres of water are pumped daily from the Tsumeb shafts, transforming an otherwise drab mining town into a leafy Eden.

65

66

67

68

69

65 A Herero woman, cool and gracious like Swakopmund itself, crosses one of the streets in this fashionable seaside resort. A pier was built here with great difficulty when Britain restricted German use of the harbour facilities at Walvis Bay. Although Swakopmund has faded from importance as a port, it continues to flourish, the gentle climate attracting streams of visitors during the summer when conditions become all but unbearable farther inland. **66** Photographed in front of buildings splashed with signs in German, a group of black South Westers epitomize something of the cosmopolitan atmosphere of Swakopmund. **67** Children wait patiently outside a Swakopmund bottle store with its bold sign touting for business in German and English. **68** Holiday-makers and townsfolk walk past the symbol of Swakopmund's famous lighthouse. **69** Very few buildings dating from the German period still stand on Kaiserstrasse, Windhoek. The steeply-pitched roofs designed to cope with heavy falls of snow strike an incongruous note in this tropical city.

70

71

72

73

74

75

76

70 Swakopmund jail, as imposing a prison as one might care to encounter yet, considering its function, not without a certain continental charm. **71** The Lutheran Church, Windhoek, mirrors a strange mixture of styles and influences. **72** African palms stand in startling contrast to the quaint half-timbered Woermann House in Swakopmund. **73** Baroque architecture in an African setting, the Lutheran Church in Swakopmund boasts a simple white tower surmounted by a fanciful double-onion pinnacle which is reminiscent of many similar buildings in southern Germany. **74** Redolent with the atmosphere of an earlier colonial period, palm-studded Swakopmund railway station from which the first passenger train left for Windhoek in June 1902. **75** A bird perches in the loft window of this building dating from the German period. **76** On the Khomas Hochland stands haunted Liebig Haus, its delapidated windows looking towards the nearby 'Trockenposten' where drunken *Schutztruppe* from Windhoek were sent to 'dry out' before resuming duty.

77

78

79

77 Fort Duwisib on the edge of the Namib Desert was built by a German baron for himself and his American wife. Despite the fort's arid desert setting the German atmosphere is all-pervasive as this corner filled with coats-of-arms, martial symbols and elaborately carved furniture shows. **78** Today South West boasts a modern postal service and a telephone system linked to South Africa's national and international exchange. However, this splendid post-office plaque recalls an earlier period. **79** In Waterberg cemetery an ornate plaque commemorates those who died in the 1904 war against the Herero. **80** A soft frame of trees and plants enfolds the Roman Catholic Church at Tsumeb.

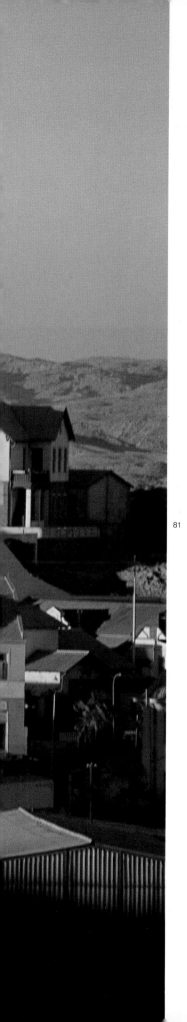

81

82

81 Barren hills echo the utter desolation of Lüderitz, a town almost completely devoid of plant-life and dependent for every drop of water it uses on a borehole at Koichab, 100 kilometres away. Lüderitz Bay was discovered by Bartholomew Diaz in 1487 when he sailed into its small rock-bound gulf on his way south to find a sea-route to India. Named Angra Pequena by Diaz, the town received its present name from its founder, Adolf Lüderitz, whose burning ambition it was to establish a German colony on the South West African coast. Second to Walvis Bay, Lüderitz Bay is the only other natural harbour of note along the entire South West African coast and its sheltered harbour is the centre of the lucrative crayfish industry. The town, despite its complete lack of fresh water, has a certain charm. The buildings have all the character and taste lacking in more utilitarian urban areas like Walvis Bay and Tsumeb, and the ubiquitous grey rocks that outcrop everywhere lend a ruggedness and abstract beauty to the setting. In the late 19th century when the town suddenly boomed with the diamond rush, fresh water was so exorbitantly expensive that old-timers claimed it was cheaper to bathe in soda water. **82** Nama children pose shyly under an arch of ornamental stonework at the Mission Church in Gibeon. The area around the town was originally inhabited by the Bergdamara who called it 'the place where the zebras drink'. Today Gibeon is the tribal centre of the Nama who settled there in the second half of the 18th century.

83

84

85

86

83 Surely one of Nature's most comic creatures when waddling pompously on the ground, is the pelican. But, once in the air, majesty returns for these great birds soar effortlessly on thermals until mere specks in the sky. To feed they use their capacious beaks as nets, often fishing together in the shallows. First they surround a shoal which, with their wings and feet, is driven into an ever-shrinking circle. Then, as if at a signal, the birds dip their membranous beaks into the water to scoop up their trapped victims. **84** A keen avian fisherman, this Grey Heron keeps a watchful eye on its human counterparts angling from the old pier at Swakopmund. **85** Dressed in a curious combination of tropical helmet, leather gloves, sandals and dark glasses, an elderly inhabitant pushes his bicycle along the mole at Swakopmund. **86** There is a saying that at Swakopmund 'the sun never rises, never sets'. On most days dawn comes slowly filtering through the thick grey fog that blankets the desert coast. The sun, an illuminated disc in the hazy air, makes its first appearance mid-morning when a sea-breeze carries the mist inland providing vital moisture for the creatures of the desert. When evening falls, the dying rays of the sun are swallowed up once more by the thickening atmosphere of the descending fog. **87** The 'Eisenbrücke', or iron jetty, favourite fishing spot for visitors and locals alike.

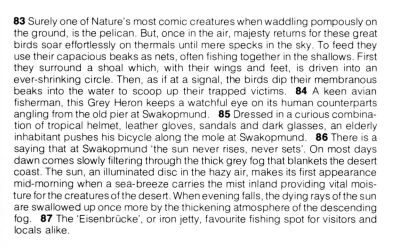

87

88

89

90

91

88 This sign speaks for itself. **89** To tame this inhospitable country, the greatest challenge has been to traverse vast distances over difficult terrain. Early transport relied on the laboriously slow ox-wagon and the journey between Walvis Bay and Windhoek took 101 exhausting hours. Then, in 1844 Jonker Afrikaner built the famous 'Bay Road', which became a vital link between the two towns. Today the situation has been greatly eased by the building of some 58 000 kilometres of road linking all the major centres in the territory. **90** This modern diesel locomotive is a far cry from the early steam engines which operated on South West's narrow-gauge railway system. An Owambo brakeman travelled on each truck; one whistle from the driver served as a warning to apply the brakes; two blasts were the signal for the brakes to be released; and three meant an emergency – for instance when game was sighted and the driver and foreman dashed out with their rifles to bag something for the pot. On other occasions it was not entirely unusual for the passengers to be ordered to collect wood when the engine began running low on fuel! **91** Dust billows behind a car travelling on one of South West's notorious 'dirt' roads.
92 Heavily subsidized, motor transport provides a vital life-line for people living in remote areas.

93

94

95

93 A Promec Drilling Jumbo Car tears at the rock-face creating a cavernous chamber to house the hydro-electric generators that will eventually be driven by the waters of the Kunene River. When complete, this colossal undertaking at Ruacana in the north will provide the whole of South West Africa with electricity. **94** Mineworkers, their yellow overalls picked out sharply against the blood-red earth, wash tailings back into mined-out shafts at Tsumeb. As a result there are none of the ugly dumps that usually stand as testimony to man's plundering of the earth. Since time immemorial the Owambo and other black peoples of South West Africa have collected copper from the rich blue-green surface outcrops at Tsumeb and smelted the almost pure ore into treasured articles of jewellery and spearheads. No longer only a copper mine, Tsumeb has turned out to be the richest source of lead and zinc in Africa; indeed the subterranean reefs nearby are composed of over 50 different rocks and minerals of untold value. **95** Construction work in progress on the tunnel at the Ruacana Hydro-electric scheme.

96

97

96 At its narrowest point a man can straddle the Sesriem Canyon on the edge of the Namib Desert. The canyon, gouged out by the occasional but violent flooding of the Tsauchab, restricts the broad river which drops dramatically and hurtles for a distance of 1,5 kilometres through the 30 metre-deep gorge. This remarkable canyon was discovered quite by chance by a farmer who tied six strips or 'riems' of ox-hide together to reach the bottom: hence the name Sesriem – literally six riems. **97** Biggest and most impressive of all the aloes is the kokerboom, the so-called quivertree, its fibrous core providing pincushion-type quivers for the Bushman hunters. Thrusting thick sappy trunks between inhospitable boulders in the kokerboom forest near Keetmanshoop in the south, these trees can withstand years of bitter drought. **98** Like a miniature African version of the Matterhorn, the 'Spitzkoppe' near Usakos. A rockhound's paradise, this area is rich in the precious and semi-precious stones for which South West is world-renowned – blue lace agate, tourmaline, amethyst, rose quartz, topaz, beryl of every colour, and exquisite mineral specimens to dazzle the eye.

99

99 Charles John Andersson wrote: 'What a wonderful effect the accidents of light and shade have on a landscape.' He could well have been describing this silent southern landscape near Narubis. **100** Not since 1934 has the Kuiseb River broken through to the sea. Photographs taken from an orbiting earth-satellite dramatically emphasised that the Kuiseb is the incisive dividing line between the rich orange dunes of the Namib on the southern bank and the bleak grey gravel plains of the northern desert. Sands that attempt to encroach north of the river are swept away each year in the Kuiseb's floodwaters, but at the river mouth the dunes have managed to race ahead. Here they have entirely blocked the river's exit to the sea and the Kuiseb's waters are forced deep beneath the sands.

101

102

101 The round bushes shown here are completely atypical of the waste strips of gravel and water-tumbled pebbles that divide successive dunes from one another in the Namib. These narrow 'streets' are aptly named, for vehicle access to the desert is easiest along these natural routes. By mutual agreement drivers carefully follow previous tracks rather than repeatedly scar the desert surface. Wind activity is minimal on the dune streets and in one remarkable case, a German gun carriage abandoned in 1914 and discovered only decades later, still had clearly visible tracks leading up to it. **102** In the primordial silence of the Kuiseb Canyon a man's heartbeat is all he hears. So still, so lifeless, this lunar landscape is called the 'gramadulas' – an expression that has become local idiom for the back side of beyond.

103

104

105

106

103 Flamingoes feast in the nutrient-rich waters that overflow from the Walvis Bay sewage works. Their much-admired pink and crimson-tinged plumage is directly linked to the pigment carotene found in the tiny brine shrimps and other marine organisms on which the birds feed. Before this was a recognised fact, flamingoes in captivity remained inexplicably white after their first moult. By trial and error, perplexed zoo-keepers finally discovered the answer: when their artificial diet was supplemented with live brine shrimps, the plumage soon reverted to its familiar rosy colour. **104** To the benefit of birds though not of man, Sandwich Harbour has gradually become silted up. Until 1912 ships anchored in its sheltered lagoon but the 8 kilometres of sand that create an almost impenetrable barrier between coast and hinterland limited its usefulness. It marks the erstwhile mouth of the Kuiseb River which today, deprived of

direct access to the sea by the encroaching desert, seeps away beneath the dunes. A lush fringe of rushes and sweet-water vegetation at the coast thrives on the seepage from the Kuiseb and harbours a rich and varied bird-life. **105** Namib desert sand seen through a microscope reveals dark-coloured garnet and bitumen particles amid the reddish iron-oxide coated grains of silica. Sculpted by water – not wind as originally thought – rounded fragments such as these overlie some 20% of South West Africa's surface. These vast quantities of sand were probably washed down to the sea by rivers and ancient flood waters, tumbled by the action of the waves, and finally deposited on the shores to be carried inland by the westerly winds that once prevailed. **106** Isolated in the bed of the Swakop River lies Goanikontes Oasis, a refreshing splash of green after the brown and yellow dryness of the desert.

107

108

107 South West Africa is a land of open space and sky – even in the massive Brandberg where the highest point in the entire country, Königstein, soars 2 579 metres into a cloudless sky.   **108** Deep in Damaraland lies Twyfelfontein, famous for its fine rock engravings made by unknown artists in times long past. Even more astounding are the engraved slabs recently discovered in the desert. Carbon-14 dating has revealed that the people of southern Africa were creating works of art at the same time as the early cave artists of Altamira.
109 As if charred by some infernal fire, the Burnt Mountain continues to puzzle visitors and scientists. Rising to 200 metres near Twyfelfontein, its crudely-shaped formations of red rock are inexplicably streaked with vivid areas of black, white and grey.

110

111

112

110 What Nature has withheld from South West Africa in conventional beauty she has more than made up in mineral wealth and throughout the territory rich deposits hold the promise of untold wealth. The giant mining industry earns approximately R230 million annually, some of which comes from small operations like this open tin mine in the Namib. **111** Measuring the acidity of slurry in a Namib lead mine. **112** In a flotation cell gleaming surface-bubbles and rich textural qualities transform this photograph into a work of art. **113** Like a weird monster this machine peers over a great mound of salt. Vast, inexhaustible salt deposits occur all along South West's coast. Near Swakopmund shallow pans are bulldozed in the sand and sea water is then pumped in, allowed to evaporate and the residual crust of salt is carefully scraped up and collected.

115

116

114 Progress demands a price, and slag from the Uis tin mine makes the point. Strip mining for this valuable mineral has defaced much of the area and even the camera's lens cannot altogether hide the slag-heap's ugly face.
115 Rusted remains of a prospector's jeep.   **116** A country dealer's tiny store at Kamanjab, Damaraland.

117

118

119

120

117 Below the distant Brandberg nestle the ramshackle dwellings of a small Bergdamara community. A mysterious negroid people, very like the Bushman in outlook, customs and way of life, the Bergdamara have long been oppressed by other tribes in South West Africa. Enslaved by the Herero and Nama, they have entirely lost their tribal identity and today only common physical characteristics identify the 75 000 or so that live in scattered family units in the arid northern parts of the territory. 118 A modern adaptation of the traditional Hottentot hut. Strongly reminiscent of the Arab nomad's tent, these huts used to be made from reeds no longer obtainable. In the hot season the shaded yet airy interior provided relief from the baking sun, and during the summer downpours the reeds, swollen with moisture, made the shelter water-tight. Hessian and corrugated iron are poor substitutes, particularly among nomadic peoples who must be able to pack up and move at short notice. 119 Instantly recognisable by his dark skin and negroid features, a Bergdamara man in western dress. 120 Legacy from times of drought, the dry cracked earth awaits sudden downpours that will almost miraculously bring it to life. Seeds lie patiently buried in the earth until, signalled by the rains, they burst forth and transform the arid land into a flowering wilderness.

121

122

121 Mbanderu men trek with their pack-horses along a dusty road near Grootfontein. According to legend the Herero migrated under two chiefs from an unknown country called Raruu in central Africa. Moving slowly south, they crossed present-day Botswana, one group, the Mbanderu, remaining near to what is today Gobabis, and the brother tribe, the Herero, moving further west to the Kaokoveld. After 200 years, the peripatetic Herero travelled south where they became locked in bloody conflict with the Nama. Although Mbanderu and Herero are ethnically related, they do not intermarry and regard themselves now as two distinctly separate peoples. **122** Goats wander along a dirt road in the Khomas Hochland, near Windhoek. Although dry for eight months of the year, this is one of the finest grazing areas in South West and the centre of a prosperous farming community.

123

124

125

126

127

It is difficult to believe that the scientists who come to the research station at Gobabeb – literally 'the place where there is nothing' – find that there is in fact a great deal there. A unique fauna has slowly evolved over many millenia in the Namib, adapting so remarkably to the hostile setting that the possibility of life on Mars does not seem far-fetched!

123 Leaving precise tracks, a sidewinding adder moves easily over the slippery Namib dunes. To hunt, it buries itself completely in the sand but for its protruding eyes set high on its head, and the black tip of its tail. Safely dug in and using the exposed tip of its tail as a lure, it will wait patiently for its prey to come within striking-distance. **124** Only in the Namib live these black and white *Onymacris bicolor* beetles, one of the five species of white tenebrionid beetles unique to this desert. Scientists now believe that the distinctive white back has evolved as an adaptation to hot desert conditions and serves to reflect some of the sun's radiant heat. In this way these beetles are able to forage on the dune-surface long after their black counterparts have tunnelled into the

sand to hide from the burning sun. The female of the species is far larger than her mate and she requires proportionately more food. It is likely, therefore, that by travelling piggy-back the male shields part of her body with his own so that she may enjoy longer feeding hours. **125** A silent member of an otherwise noisy family, the *Palmatogecko* gorges on a luckless grasshopper. Padding stealthily on its webbed feet, the gecko is a nocturnal hunter, shunning the daylight hours when the sun would scorch its fragile skin. **126** In the Namib only the fittest survive, and in the desert context few creatures are more feared than the spiders and scorpions. Here a 15 cm long thick-tailed scorpion makes short work of a grasshopper. **127** A family of suricates pose as if for a formal portrait. **128** The subject of endless speculation since discovered in 1918, the White Lady of Brandberg still puzzles archaeologists. She is almost certainly neither white nor a lady, and the theory that she reflects Cretan or Egyptian influences is unlikely, although why the figure is so much larger than the surrounding ones and differs so markedly from them has not yet been satisfactorily explained.

129   130   131

Diverted from the main stream that swirls from west to east around Antarctica, the Benguela Current moves like a cold murky river along South West Africa's desert coast. Clearly defined from the warmer Atlantic Ocean, this narrow belt of water brings a double blessing to the land: the sea mists that tame the fury of the tropical sun; and the wealth of sea-life that flourishes on its rich nutrients. In a remarkable food chain born in the chemical-laden ice floes of the Antarctic, plankton feed and multiply, their numbers turning the sea into a lead-coloured meadow on which large shoals of fish pasture. What these shoals may lack in variety is more than compensated for by the sheer overwhelming numbers of fish like pilchards and maasbankers which form the basis of South West Africa's lucrative fishing industry. In competition with man for this food supply is a prolific bird-life – penguins, cormorants and gannets feed hungrily on its bounty, in part repaying man's loss by the valuable layer of guano they deposit on their breeding sites.

129 The sea in their blood, fishermen of the west coast harvest waters that teem with pilchards, maasbankers and anchovies. 1947 marked the beginning of the fishing industry on a large scale. As an incentive to fishermen the companies offered them loans to buy boats allowing them to repay the debt in terms of their catches. With its head-quarters at Walvis Bay, the industry earned R88 million in 1975 from canned fish, fish meal and fish oil. Tonnage figures fluctuate yearly for reasons not clearly understood, but it would appear that some ecological imbalance plays a part – together with the uncontrolled catches made by trawlers from other countries that pirate South West's waters.   **130** A satisfied fisherman, proud master of his vessel, his hold bursting with a catch that will earn him R22 per ton.   **131** Preparing for the next season, a fisherman mends the fine nets which will trap the smaller fish like anchovies that have recently made their appearance off South West Africa's coast. **132** A fisherman relaxes with cigarette in hand while the day's catch is offloaded from the hold.

133

134

135

136

133 A suction pipe (bottom right) draws pilchards from a trawler's hold.
134 The slippery, silvery mass of fish is carried by conveyor belt directly from the dock to the factory. The machine in the background automatically measures the catch and its tally dictates what each fisherman will earn for his labours. **135** Owambo workers in the Wesco canning factory at Walvis Bay, centre of the west coast fishing industry. **136** The fish are running! Seen through a maze of chains and ropes, boats about to leave for the fishing grounds.

137

138

137 Spruce in white overalls, factory workers pack whole rock-lobster for export, mainly to Japan. Crayfish tails find a ready market – and high prices – in the USA where southern African 'crawfish' are a particular delicacy. **138** In a glorious interplay of primary colours, this fisherman manoeuvres his dory among the crayfish pots to collect the catch. The crayfish squirming in the bottom of his boat will be transferred to the nearby trawlers that carry them to Lüderitz Bay, centre of the South West crayfish industry.

139

140

139 Corroded by salt air, a blubber pot crumbles beside a long-discarded anchor and bleached whale-bones at Cape Cross. As far back as the 1700s English and American whalers operated off the coast, decimating the leviathans that flourished in the plankton-rich sea. At what are today Swakopmund and Walvis Bay they set up small settlements where they melted down the blubber so precious in the days before the earth's mineral oil reserves were known. The whales hopelessly over-exploited and their oil now largely displaced by the oilfields' cheaper product, whaling is a dying industry on southern Africa's west coast. **140** Desiccated by salt and sun, a seal wears a gruesome death-smile. **141** A ship wrecked on the dreaded Skeleton Coast 'where ships and men come ashore to die'. Treacherous seas and shifting sands make this one of the most dangerous coasts in the world. Countless ships have foundered here, their broken hulks buried and then exposed by the restless desert sands. Those sailors who miraculously escaped death in the sea soon perished on the unforgiving shore, their vessel like their lives forfeited to Nature.

142

142 Rocks encrusted with barnacles. **143** Confidently dating the creation of the world at 5200 BC, the black granite replica of Diego Cão's original *padrão* at Cape Cross states in Latin and Portuguese: 'Since the creation of the world 6684 years have passed, and since the birth of Christ 1484 years, and so the Illustrious Don Johannes has ordered this pillar to be erected here by Jacobus Canus, his knight.' **144** On the night of 29 November 1942 the ill-fated British liner *Dunedin Star* ran aground off the Skeleton Coast. A rude shock awaited the 63 passengers who managed to reach land; the desert offered no more promise than the watery grave they had been 'fortunate' to escape. Rescue operations were successful but one of the Ventura bombers taking part became bogged down in the sand and had to be abandoned, this engine remaining as a lone reminder.

146

145 In anachronistic but spectacular dress, Herero women join the annual pilgrimage to the graves of three great chiefs, Tjamuaha (d 1859), Maharero (d 1890) and Samuel Maharero (d 1923). On the last Sunday in August each year, Herero flock to Okahandja (Great Place of the Herero) near Windhoek to pay their respects to the dead and reinforce their national unity.   **146** A Herero woman in full regalia, her dark skin a perfect foil for the brilliant white of her headdress and sombre gown. To enhance their already considerable charms some Herero women include in their *toilette* brown boot polish dabbed on the cheeks and 'polished' to an attractive shine. German missionaries of the 19th century influenced many of the scantily dressed indigenous tribes to adopt European clothing and, in the case of the Herero, this distinctive dress has become a symbol of national identity.

147

148

149

147 Her skirt a work of art and the result of countless hours' labour, this Herero woman wears typical flowing skirt, immaculately tied head-cloth and graceful leg-o'-mutton sleeves. Tall and haughty, the Herero women walk with a slow measured stride that dates to an earlier time when their arms and legs were weighed down with heavy brass rings. In time of war these rings became prized booty and were efficiently removed by simply chopping off a limb.
148 Not to be overshadowed by their womenfolk, Herero men decked out in 'uniform' on Maharero's Day. **149** Seated between two loyal tribesmen, a

150

Herero chief poses for a formal photograph. The Herero are a conservative and proud people. Traditionally herders, they attach most value to the cattle on which a man's status and prestige are judged. The large herds are carefully tended and killed only on ceremonial occasions or as part of funerary rites. **150** Red-band Herero, those related to Samuel Maharero, at the Okahandja festivities. The ceremony centres on two important religious symbols: the graves of the ancestor-chiefs, and the sacred fire that epitomizes in its perpetual glow the continued existence and prosperity of the people.

151

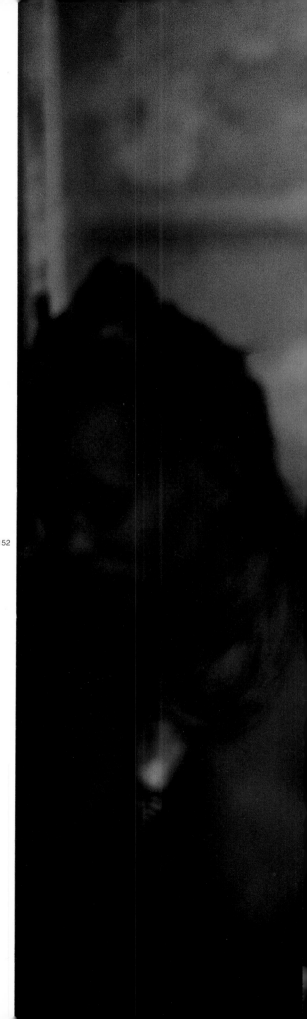

152

151 Imbued with quiet dignity, a Himba woman and her child wait outside a local clinic in the Kaokoveld. The large whelk shell that hangs about her slender neck is a popular adornment with both men and women of this tribe. Virtually untouched by Western culture, for over a century they have completely rejected the missionaries who sought to work among them. They have clung stubbornly to the ways of their ancestors and, whereas the Herero of which the Himba are a clan, have embraced much of Western culture and dress, the Himba have changed little since the 16th century. In about 1550, when the Herero clans reached what is now South West Africa in their southward migration, the first to cross the Kunene River were the Tjimba who lost their cattle in this arid country and were condemned to a life of hunting and gathering. The Himba fared better, keeping their cattle and adopting the Tjimba as servants – to their mutual benefit. By tradition goat and cattle breeders, the Himba, by the very nature of their aloof and forbidding land, keep their kraals small and must look to the insects and plants of the desert to supplement their diet. Cattle, as with most Bantu-speaking people, are sacrosanct and the Himba slaughter them only for sacrifice to the ancestors, which are not 'worshipped' as is often thought, but regarded as extensions of the living world. The dead are believed to take an active interest in the affairs of their kith and kin and, if displeased, can bring misfortune. **152** Proud, beautiful and supremely feminine, a Himba woman decked in finery commensurate with her looks. Below her weighty necklaces hangs a whelk shell, a prized item of jewellery.

153   154

153 Himba women smeared from head to foot in a mixture of butter and ochre. Undisturbed by the decidedly rancid smell of this cosmetic, they consider it essential to their appearance and claim, furthermore, that it protects them from the sun's piercing rays. For good grooming, every part of the body and every item of dress must be anointed with this mixture which is worn by men and women alike. **154** A study in earth-tones, a Himba woman feeds her child. She is wearing the headdress of a married woman, the hair of the crown of her head pulled and twisted around sisal threads, heavily buttered and then dressed with the ochre beloved by these people. The heavy strands of coiled and plaited hair are then surmounted by a goatskin frill that is a further symbol of her married status. Disdaining cheap glass beads and Western ornaments, the Himba fashion belts and necklaces from leather studded with home-made beads of shell and ivory. The heavy brass rings adorn this woman's arms permanently and hark back to the Herero practice of earlier times.

155

155 A Himba youth coaxes a plaintive song from his simple mouth harp. Hair-styles among the Himba, as with many African tribes, are varied and allow for some degree of individuality, but their basic form is dictated by status and at a glance tells much about the wearer. In this case the single pigtail and otherwise clean-shaven head immediately show that this young man is not yet married. **156** Himba boys and girls relax in the scant shade of a tree. The youth on the right adopts a characteristic 'resting' stance, one leg draped across the other. Sandals protect their feet from the baking sand and European belts and a T-shirt are obvious innovations; but the girls' dress is purely traditional. **157** Perched behind this married Himba's ear and only partly

156

157

158

159

visible is a spoon-like 'head scratcher', much needed under his well-buttered and ochred headdress. The turban covers two thick oily plaits of hair which become hot and sticky under the sun. **158** A Himba chief's grave surrounded by stones, stout poles and the horns of cattle sacrificed at the funeral. To ensure that the spirit of the sacrificial beast does not escape its body when the mourners break its neck with their bare hands, its nostrils are stuffed with grass and clay and its mouth held shut. The dead person's body is bound up in the raw hide and lowered in a crouching position into the grave, together with his personal belongings. The mourning that follows is long and uninhibited, and to ensure that the ancestors welcome the new member into their ranks,

offerings of raw meat are made. Once the funerary rites are over the grave becomes a solemn shrine, the ground hallowed and the place one of worship. **159** Water, more precious in the desert than any diamond, is for drinking only; indeed, washing is traditionally taboo and believed to bring bad luck on the hunt. Against a background of the simple werfs that form the Bushman's home, a woman watches her child drink from an ostrich shell. The Bushmen store water, when it is available, in these shells which they then seal with beeswax and hide in the cool depths of the sand. Bringing relief when all other water supplies are gone, are the small caches of this life-giving liquid that lie buried at secret spots known only to the Bushmen themselves.

160 Like a desert gazelle, a Bushman girl casts her eyes down demurely before the camera's lens. Her smooth golden complexion is the trophy of youth, for soon the dry desert air will prematurely wrinkle her skin and, lacking the adipose tissue normal to other races, it will soon fall in folds about her.
161 Her eyes closed in pleasure, a woman draws deeply on her metal pipe. Tobacco is the Bushman's greatest luxury, tempting him from his desert fastnesses to barter egg-shell beads and soft curried skins for this treasured weed. Now largely restricted to the remote areas of the Kalahari, Bushmen were the earliest people to roam southern Africa's vast plains. Defeated later by the hordes of Bantu-speaking tribes that surged down from the north in search of fresh grazing, the diminutive Bushman was forced to adapt to life in areas too inhospitable for the newcomers. Here they live to this day, in perfect harmony with their surroundings. Named by themselves 'the harmless people', they have learnt that to survive they must repress all aggression and what at first appears as weakness is in fact their strength. **162** Squatting on her haunches Bushman-style, a young mother suckles her baby. Dressed only in a leather apron and skin kaross over one shoulder, she carries her child easily on the left hip as custom demands. Survival necessitates harsh rules; for instance, if twins are born the younger will be put to death – as will a baby whose mother dies in childbirth. Among these primitive hunters and gatherers there is no question of morality here; each person must contribute something to the family unit as it wanders the desert vastness and to place an unnatural burden on the group as a whole is indeed to threaten its very survival. While the men hunt, the women and children roam the seemingly fruitless land, their sharp eyes picking up tell-tale signs of moisture-filled tubers and succulent roots below ground. Using digging sticks, they work the earth loose to find their prize and carry the day's harvest back to the werfs. When all else fails, the tsamma melon can always be relied upon. It provides moisture to drink and oil in its seeds. To prepare this dish the Bushmen open the top, mash the soft pulp with a stick and then with much satisfied grunting swallow the contents.

163

164

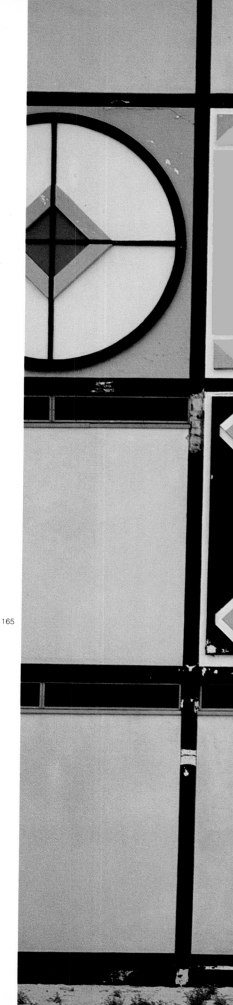

165

163 From time immemorial, primitive man – including the Bushman – has made fire by rubbing sticks together and catching the sparks on a dry tuft of grass. On bitterly cold nights fires burn brightly beside every skerm (shelter) and the members of the family curl close about its embers for warmth – so close that many a shin bears scars from the hot ashes! **164** Music is close to the Bushman's soul. This man plays the *guashi,* a popular instrument among these people. His bow and arrow are superb hunting tools, the arrow-tips smeared with a deadly poison made from the grubs of the *Diamphidia simplex.* Tireless hunters, they stalk their prey with animal cunning and will jog many kilometres after a wounded beast. A successful hunt means meat for all and the group will gorge itself until no scrap remains. A small quantity may be dried for another day, but the Bushman's philosophy does not provide for the future and with supreme optimism the people enjoy today's fruit today and trust in their ability to survive on whatever Nature will provide on the morrow. **165** Bold graphics in the African idiom, the Owambo teachers' training college at Ongwediva.

166

167

168

166 Insurance against leaner times, salted bream dry on the roof of an Owambo hut. The dehydrated fish will eventually be ground to paste with water and added, mainly as flavouring, to the sorghum (durra) porridge that is the Owambo's staple food. Living on the rolling grassy plains south of the Kunune River, the Owambo are the largest single population group (396 000) in South West. They consist of eight kindred matrilineal Bantu tribes, each with its own dialect and customs but having similar origins.   **167** Owambo girls fish with *shikuku* reed baskets, during the floods that spread over wide tracts of land each summer. Rivers burst their banks and pools and puddles grow larger until they link up like beads on a necklace. At this time of year fishing becomes the focus of activity, one in which men, women, girls and boys all take part, laughing and singing together as they work. The *shikuku* is popular with women who create a barrage with their baskets and, having chased the fish into the shallows, thrust again and again into the muddy waters. A tell-tale rustle inside warns of a catch and the women then slip an arm through the aperture at the top of the basket, groping for their trapped victim. Triumphantly, they toss the fish on to the bank to be promptly skinned and gutted for the pot.   **168** A fishing trap forms a canopy about an Owambo woman's head. Laid side by side in the water, these reed baskets trap fish which the Owambo drive towards the barrage, beating the water and singing all the while.

169 Laid out with almost geometric precision, an Owambo village appears isolated among the freshly sprouting fields. A stockade of mopani poles 3 metres high surrounds the village and marks out the labyrinthine passages, hardly a metre wide, that link huts and homesteads in a confusing maze. The stranger feels completely lost in these passages that eventually lead to a large central area where people meet, entertain guests and feed the sacred fire that is never allowed to die. Day and night it is tended for its light represents the well-being of the chief and his people. Villages are relatively small, 20 huts on average.

170 To a steady beat, youngsters prepare millet in the traditional manner, first sifting it in baskets and then pounding it in the deep-throated wooden mortars. Of all the indigenous peoples in South West, only the Owambo are cultivators. However, cattle do play a significant part in their lives. Like those of most Bantu-speaking people, the Owambo's herds are a great source of prestige and wealth. **171** Crafts developed into a fine art over many years, pottery and basket-weaving are acknowledged Owambo skills. The large pots in the fore-ground are to hold the opaque white beer enjoyed by most black peoples in southern Africa. This strong-smelling fermented liquid has great nutritional value – not to mention alcoholic kick! Behind the little girl is a woven storage basket in which the Owambo keep grain out of reach of insects and rats.
172 Discovered in 1901 by George Hartman, the Kunene River plunges 72 metres over the Ruacana Falls into a narrow gorge. The present name is a corruption of the lyrical Owambo name, *Oruha Hahahana,* meaning the place of hurrying waters.

173

174

173 From the air, salt-etched water-courses form elaborate patterns near Etosha Pan. Believed to have been a lake in some distant age, the entire pan is now an area of inland drainage. Over thousands of years mineral salts washed down by annual rains and floods have concentrated here leaving a thick alkaline crust when the waters evaporate during the dry season. **174** Incongruous beside a lone Makelani palm, Namutoni Fort is perhaps the most sought-after rest camp in the Etosha Game Park. Once scene of a bloody battle between seven German soldiers and a force of 500 armed Owambo, and later the centre of German administration, the fort has had a chequered history. Now, after having suffered complete neglect for many years, it has been restored to its full former splendour.

175

175 Dawn over Etosha from the heights of Namutoni Fort, where years ago that incorrigible Afrikaner band of Thirstland Trekkers settled temporarily in their endless search for Utopia in what must surely be a most unlikely quarter of the world. **176** The sky infused with soft colour, as the sun sets at Etosha. Charles John Andersson, the famous Swedish pioneer and explorer, came upon Etosha Pan in 1857 and marvelled at the teeming game that congregated near its waters. Between that time and 1907, when the Etosha was proclaimed a protected area, the creatures of the pan suffered at the merciless hand of disease and from the thoughtless depredations of man. Of course this has now changed. In its 22 000 square kilometre sanctuary roam herds of zebra, antelope, wildebeest and giraffe among a host of other species; lion, hyena, cheetah and leopard stalk the plains in search of prey; birds reap the water's harvest. Etosha is also the home of the rarest antelope in the world, the Black-faced Impala, whose timid ways and gentle beauty would be lost to the world if it were not protected in the park. For those who visit it, Etosha provides an experience never to be forgotten.

177

178

179

177 Raising a fine film of pink-tinted dust, a group of Burchell's zebra stamp their hooves in Etosha's chill morning air. **178** While a lone gemsbok looks on, zebras skirmish and butt on the dusty plain. **179** Drinking thirstily of Etosha's mineral-rich but salty waters, zebra, springbok and Crested Guinea-fowl keep peaceful company.

180

181

182

183

180 Wildebeest amble towards a waterhole. According to Bushman legend the wildebeest was intended by God to look like a buffalo – hence the powerful head and shoulders. But when it came to finishing the job, He was in a hurry and slapped on the rather indifferent hindquarters.   **181** Silhouettes at a waterhole – giraffe beside the tenement-block nests of weavers.   **182** Early travellers record springbok herds so vast that they could be seen trekking past without a break from sunrise to sunset. Not so today, although the springbok are still numerous. They have been decimated by hunters and tens of thousands perished in inexplicable suicide treks to the coast when, driven by some fierce instinctive urge, they threw themselves violently into the sea to drown.
183 Toy of the Etosha, the Damara Dik-dik, a tiny buck weighing no more than 5 kilograms and with hooves the size of a human fingernail. The large gland clearly visible at the corner of the dik-dik's eye oozes a secretion that the male deposits at the edge of his territory to claim ownership and warn off rivals.

184

185

186

187

188

184 Life is one long meal for the elephant, which must stolidly eat its way through about 150 kilograms of food, washed down by some 150 litres of water, daily. To consume these quantities the adult spends at least 16 hours of the day satisfying its stomach, and the rest sleeping and enjoying the pleasures of a mudbath. In contrast to the muddy elephants wallowing in the background, the large beast in front appears white from the encrustation of mineral salts from another waterhole. **185** Famous for its spurts of incredible speed, the cheetah is now an endangered species. Although definitely a member of the cat family, it has curiously dog-like unretractable claws. **186** Fragile ears cupped to catch every sound, this Impala ewe stopped barely long enough to be caught on film. With the click of the shutter she was off into the dry bush and within seconds lost from view. **187** A Striped Ground Squirrel suckles her young. These rodents adapt well to the arid surroundings and normally carry their bushy tails along their backs to act as an umbrella over the animal's delicate spine. **188** Master of all it surveys, a lion lazes under a tropical sun at Etosha Game Reserve.

189

189 Nyangara, the oldest mission station on the Okavango River, was founded by the Roman Catholic Church in 1909. Boasting a superbly equipped hospital, the mission supplies most of its needs from the fertile land. **190** Goats traipse across a sere Kaokoveld landscape. Strikingly different from the rest of South West Africa, this remote north-western region is one of wild barren mountains and flat grey plains. Few people live here and those that do – the Himba, Tjimba, Damara and Bushman – follow a primitive way of life in keeping with the impoverished environment.

191

192

193

194

195

196

191 Nuns pause to chat at Nyangara Mission. **192** Lush riverine forest clings to the banks of the Kunene River just above Epupa Falls. **193** An Owambo woman in the traditional headdress of marriage. From puberty the girls begin to stretch their naturally frizzy hair into amazingly long strands. Using copious amounts of butter and twisted fibre, they prepare themselves for the day when they, too, will earn the right to put their hair up in this elaborate style. **194** A sporty cockade matching the twinkle in his eye, an Owambo man near Andara Mission. **195** Moving slowly through the north-eastern part of the territory flows the Okavango River on whose banks the Roman Catholic Church erected Andara Mission. The river descends from the Angolan highlands to feed the spreading marshes of the Okavango swamps and then drains away beneath the Kalahari's dull red sands. Owambo is the most heavily populated part of South West, for here the rains are good and the earth fertile. **196** Only 129 kilometres downstream from the Ruacana Falls the Kunene River plunges yet again to drop 36 metres over the lip of the Epupa Falls. Thundering down a narrow chasm a mere 6 metres wide, the water boils with constant violence.

197

198

197 A dug-out barely causes ripples on the surface as it slips across Lake Liambezi in the Caprivi. The Caprivi Zipfel is a curious finger of territory protruding due east from Kavango to the Zambezi some 482 kilometres away. The strip, no more than 80 kilometres wide, was ceded by Britain to Germany in 1893 when imperialism was at its zenith. Theoretically it was to link South West with German East Africa, but Cecil John Rhodes's annexation of Rhodesia interfered with the plan and the corridor got no further than the Zambezi River. **198** Perfectly at home on the water, the people of the Okavango freely traverse its waters to visit one another, fish and trade. **199** Before the cleansing rains, a thick layer of dust coats roadside vegetation a ghostly grey.

200

201

202

203

204

205

200 A mopani tree gripped in the coils of a 'python climber' also known as the strangler fig'. **201** West of Okaukuejo in the Etosha National Park is the haunted forest, a strange place where *Moringa ovalifolia* seem to thrust stumpy roots skywards. Bushmen legend attributes trees like these to the god hora who, when gardening in paradise, decided that they were too ugly to nclude. Dissatisfied, he pulled them out, in the process pricking himself on heir thorns. Then, in a fit of pique, he tossed them over the wall of paradise and hey crashed to earth in South West Africa, many of them upside down with heir branches buried in the sand! **202** A tranquil view across the Kunene River into Angola. **203** Scattered into a small enclosure just west of Xhorixas, n Damaraland, lie a large number of fossilized trees. Some 200 million years old, the trees of the petrified forest are believed to have been borne by oodwaters to this area millenia ago. In the same area the primitive Welwitschia lant is found, a 'living fossil' among the dead. **204** The mystery of Marienfluss perfect circles of bare soil neatly surrounded by dry desert grass. One theory, s yet unproven, is that the deadly poisonous *Euphorbia* once grew in these barren patches and when it finally succumbed to drought or disease it left a ainted spot where no other plant can survive. **205** The *Aloe pillansii,* a close elative of the kokerboom.

206

207

206 Warped and gnarled by the struggle for survival, trees of the desert stand bravely above a terrain so inhospitable that little else dares show itself during the long hot summers. This *Sterculia quinqueloba* perches on the edge of a cliff, its smooth snow-white bark shining from afar – and at the same time reflecting some of the damaging radiant heat of the sun.   **207** Each twisted root a triumph over adversity, this desert fig tree took many years to attain its present size.   **208** A tree blossoms in the rugged landscape of the Kaokoveld.

210

209

211

212

213

214

209 Vast tracts of African savannah are scorched each year by veld fires that sweep ravenously over the land. Man is only sometimes responsible; more often lightning or some other natural accident is to blame. 210 The bushveld of the Western Caprivi; flat and sparsely covered, the summer rains will transform it into a spreading flood-plain. 211 During the Nama raids at the end of the 19th century, members of the Tjimba tribe retreated into the thankless fastnesses of the Baynes Mountains in the Kaokoveld. This desolate range was named after a certain Maudslay Baynes who, in quest of adventure in 1912, travelled on foot down the Kunene River – and a journey which began in the spirit of a picnic developed into a desperate struggle for survival. En route he discovered the mountains that bear his name, but crippled by malaria and dysentery he did not care to linger. He finally made his way to Swakopmund and thence returned to the gentler clime of Britain's shores. 212 Originally imported from Mexico, sisal flourishes in its adoptive home – in this case the Kavango area in north-eastern South West Africa. 213 Cattle draw a sledge in Kavango, where muddy conditions for a good part of the year and primitive roads give runners a decided advantage over wheels. 214 The Erongo Mountains, original home of the Bergdamara people.

215

215 Along the Okavango River, Makelani palms rustle in the softening evening breeze beneath one of the glorious sunsets special to this area. Only those who have witnessed the spectacle can believe that Nature alone has tinted these breath-taking colours. The early explorer Charles John Andersson described it: 'I remember . . . just after the sun had disappeared, the whole region of the sky, near and on the verge of the horizon, assuming exactly the resemblance of a rainbow; there were all the colours composing the glorious arch, but the ''stripes'' were three times as broad as those seen in the bow of promise . . . It was a strangely beautiful pageant.'

216

216 Makelani palms on the Okavango River. The Kavango people, a settled and long-established community, are among the most colourful of the indigenous South West African tribes. Since the early 1900s the work of missionaries has delicately blended Western practices with tribal life, particularly in the sphere of religion. Once a year the statue of the Madonna is borrowed from neighbouring Angola for an elaborate *Corpus Christi* procession. After the celebration the statue is returned aboard a splendidly decorated canoe. The entire community joyously line the wooded banks to watch the colourful procession go by. **217** The Baobab, monarch of Africa's trees.

218

219

220

218 In his bright nuptial attire a Red Bishop surveys his territory. Only during the breeding season does he risk losing his camouflage; for the rest of the year he resembles his rather dowdy brown mate. Besides his good looks and noisy courting display during which he flies bumble-bee fashion over his domain, the male Red Bishop offers his prospective mates a comfortable nest, a good food supply near by, and his ever-vigilant presence. **219** The Namaqua Sandgrouse, known affectionately as *kelkie-wyn,* come for their evening drink at a waterhole. A diet restricted to seeds is a dry one, and these small birds must always live within flying distance of water. At dawn and dusk they assemble in their hundreds to drink. When they have nestlings hidden in the desert dunes, the adult birds saturate their specially adapted breastfeathers with water and take this back to their thirsty offspring which release the moisture by nibbling at the parent's breast. **220** Wings splayed with effort, a Kori Bustard flies strongly and well – when forced to. Bustards are the heaviest of all flying birds and they burn up precious energy in becoming airborne. They prefer to stride purposefully over the arid land, eating whatever they find – be it animal or vegetable, carrion or alive – all the while keeping a wary look-out over the low scrub for approaching predators. **221** As if revolting looks and nasty disposition were not enough, the Marabou's legs are covered with a white layer of faeces. Why it defecates directly on to its legs was the subject of controversy: one theory was that the strongly alkaline waste-matter acted as a disinfectant for that part of the bird most likely to be tainted by carrion in the course of the bird's gastronomic adventures, but today the accepted theory is that this helps regulate the Marabou's temperature.

222

223

224

225

226

227

228

222 A member of the *Ornithogalum* genus, this beautiful lily is deadly poisonous to man and beast. After the first rains of summer these bulbs push urgently through the earth, thrusting aside pebbles and stones to sprout a fragile canopy of lethal blossom. **223** With a certain wild beauty of its own, the *Hermbstaedtia odorata* is a relative of the popular cockscomb. **224** Its gay flower and glossy leaves in contrast to the earth-baked soil, this plant is a member of the hibiscus family *(Malvaceae)*. **225** Related to the frangipani, the impala lily brings grace to an otherwise harsh habitat. **226** Puffs of yellow against a cloudless deep blue sky, an *Acacia millifera ssp detinens* hides cruel thorns beneath its summer flowers. *'Detinens'* means detaining, and the spiky thorns do not let you go once you are caught. **227** The spiny character of this *Hirpicium gorterioides* is a predominant feature among the daisies of South West Africa. **228** Widespread throughout tropical Africa is the flame lily, scarlet arabesques of splendid colour against the lush greenery.

229
230

229 A lonely beetle clambers over the glaucous female cones of a *Welwitschia bainesii.* This curious plant is unique, the only one of its genus, and found from the Kuiseb River northwards to southern Angola. The monstrous body, standing no more than 2 metres tall, is surrounded by a tangled mass of narrow 'leaves' and dried-out leaf-tips. But, what at first appear to be dozens of lank strap-like leaves hanging from the top of the plant, are in fact only two, each one shredded by desert winds into ribbons 2 metres long. Drawing on the desert fog for much of its liquid, the Welwitschia absorbs a certain amount of moisture through pores on its leaves. It may well be that, in addition droplets of water condensed from the fog roll easily down the drooping leaves to feed a fine network of tiny surface roots. Below ground the Welwitschia resembles a huge carrot, with a central woody core thrusting almost 3 metres into the soil. Quite obviously the air provides a more regular lifespring of water than the

231 232

233 234

earth, for a mass of rootlets ascend from the central taproot and reach the surface to find moisture there. **230** Like visitors from a distant planet, Welwitschia sprawl on the desert floor. In this desolate habitat these living fossils have clung to life for hundreds of years – some of the plants still living today doubtless date back to the birth of Christ. Maturity comes slowly, but then time is not in issue – the age of some 'young' plants has been accurately fixed at 500 or 600 years. **231** The *Tribulus zeyheri* (more commonly, the *duiweltjie* or *duwweltjie*) is a delight to the eye but a cause of concern to farmers. The young shoots contain prussic acid and sheep that eat them often die from the poison. **232** A handsome yellow-flowered legume of the desert. **233** Alone in a parched vista of cracked clay, *Datura innoxia* adapts easily and well to habitats as unfriendly as this. A native of Central America, this successful weed has spread throughout the world.

234 *Hoodia gordonii*, also called the 'carrion flower' because of the smell of putrefying flesh given off by its salmon-pink blooms. The unpleasant odour attracts flies which lay their eggs in the 10 centimetre-wide flower and pollinate the plant in the process. The Nama refer to it as the *Bobbejaan Ngaap* meaning baboon food, but this is general a term of disparagement, not a literal description. For people who lead a precarious existence in hostile surroundings, food is a major preoccupation – searching for it fills most of the day and conversation centres round it. Food is also a constant source of anxiety and therefore they scorn anything inedible. Every one of the hundreds of different plants that make up 'veldkos' has a name, but when questioned about things that cannot be eaten, the Nama's invariable reply is: 'Oh, that is baboon's food' – indicating not that these creatures necessarily eat it, but proclaiming rather their disdain.

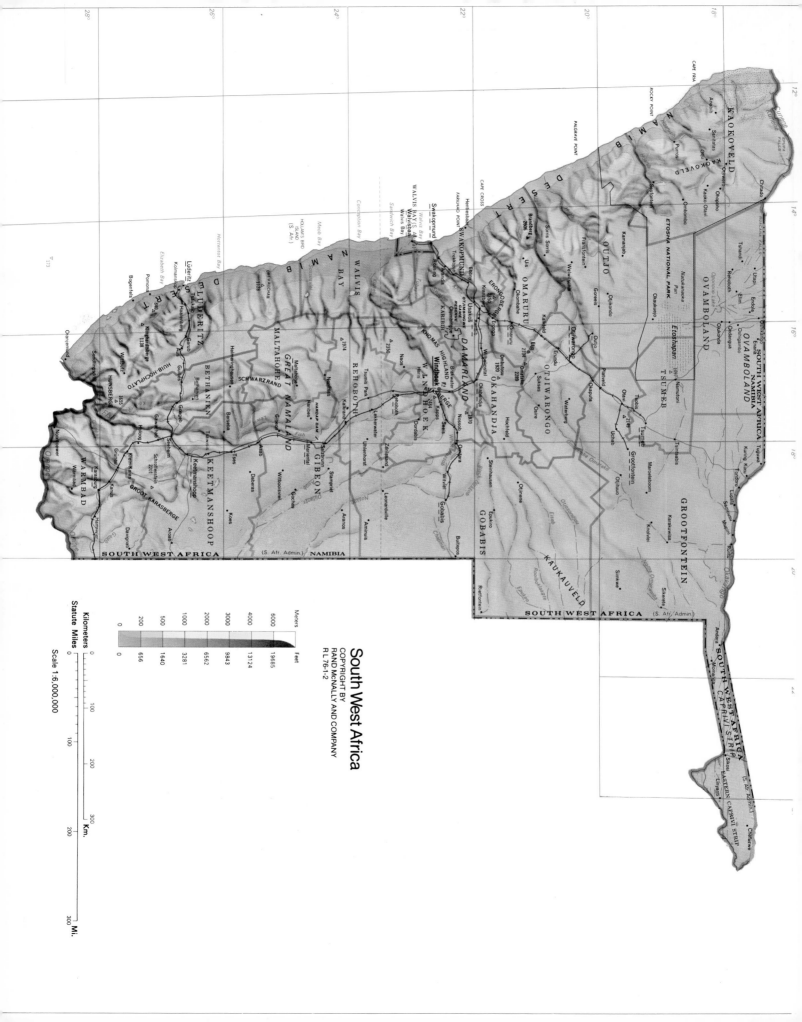

South West Africa

Scale 1:6,000,000

Meters	Feet
6000	19685
4000	13124
3000	9843
2000	6562
1000	3281
500	1640
200	656
0	0

Kilometers
Statute Miles